Best Wishes

David Lloyd.

Spirit
of the Rose

Spirit of the Rose

David Lloyd and Annie Beagent

Foreword by Dick Balfour MBE, DHM

Photographs by David Lloyd

SPIRIT OF THE ROSE

Spirit of the Rose

Project Director – David Lloyd
Project Director – Annie Beagent
Design and Production – Eddie Ephraums, Ephraums Publishing Services
Text Editor – Jill Grayston
Text copyright © Spirit of the Rose Limited
Photography copyright © David Lloyd

A catalogue record for this book is available from the British Library.
ISBN No 09543939-0-2

First published in the United Kingdom in 2004 by Spirit of the Rose Ltd
37 Woodlands, Witney, Oxfordshire OX28 2DR.

Scanning by Elizabeth Whiting Associates.
Printed in Spain, by Imago.

Dedication

This book is dedicated to Vince, a wonderful companion whose journey was tragically cut short, but who inspired me throughout. His spirit lives on through Susie, Nikki, Robyn, Reece, Peta and Vince's father Tish.
David.

"I know that for me, to whom flowers are part of desire, there are tears waiting in the petals of some rose."

Oscar Wilde: De Profundis

Acknowledgements

The publishers would like to thank all the floral designers, stylists, garden owners, breeders and contributors for all their generous and kind assistance in the creation of this project. We most sincerely apologise to those who contributed designs that were not used, and those whose gardens time and weather would not allow us to visit.

I would like to give a special thank you to Mandy, Simon, Sasha, Jon and Charlie for the freedom and encouragement to pursue this dream.
David.

A big thank you to Keith, Angela and Lizzie Parker for all their help and support with Rose text, verse and names.

Another big thank you goes to Ben and Jess for believing in the project , my mother and father, Jeanette, Diane (props department), Cliff and Nilgun for their support, and encouragement.
Annie.

All photographs were taken on Fujifilm using Hasselblad, Pentax 6X7 and SINAR 5x4" cameras, often mixing daylight with Bowens Flash and Beard tungsten lighting.

Identification of roses is not easy and the following quote from Barbara Pollard of Abbey House Gardens gives some insight into the problems many of us experience: 'We labelled everything when we planted but, the labels – small and discreet – proved infinitely pocketable, although the blackbirds tossed several around while worm hunting and we trod on a few when weeding!'

Several of the roses in this book are known by more than one name. Those alternative names may be trade names or synonyms and may differ from country to country. Many of the roses have been growing in gardens for many years and whilst the publishers have attempted to name every rose, it has not always been possible to confirm identification. The American Rose Society is the official registrar for new roses and this may mean that a few names, or the way they are written, may differ.

Contents

Foreword

Dick Balfour
R C Balfour MBE, DHM
Past President The Royal National Rose Society, President Emeritus The World Federation of Rose Societies, Past Master The Worshipful Company of Gardeners

I was greatly honoured to be invited to write the Foreword to this delightful book, one that I am confident will be treasured by all who love roses. My first thought was how much Her Majesty Queen Elizabeth The Queen Mother would have enjoyed this book. She was the Patron of The Royal National Rose Society for nearly 40 years and took a great interest in the Society. In many ways she personified the Spirit of the Rose. A keen and knowledgeable gardener with a great love of roses, her late Majesty appreciated their value and versatility as garden plants and how well they associate with other companion plants.

I was fortunate to meet her on many occasions, at the Chelsea Flower Show, on her visits to prize-winning school gardens under the aegis of the London Children's Flower Society, and at The Friends Services in St. Paul's Cathedral. For many years I made a posy of roses and other flowers from our garden for presentation to her and we talked about the flowers in the posy. One year I had included the rose Silver Jubilee and as soon as I mentioned that rose, she said, 'Wasn't it sad that he died (meaning Alec Cocker, breeder of that particular rose) and isn't it wonderful that his widow has kept the business going' – an example of her great knowledge of roses. It is indeed appropriate that this book includes the history of the Cocker dynasty.

Spirit of the Rose is beautifully illustrated with David's photographs and includes contributions from or about so many rose friends. Each contributor adds their own special interpretation of the Spirit of the Rose, its history, inspiration and symbolism, its role in art and literature, in love and war, medicine and myth, scent and science, in the language of flowers and in garden design nationwide, of castles and cottages, cities and villages. I was especially pleased to read the tribute to Julia Clements, the doyenne of flower arranging, who has had three roses named after her. Others, from royalty to sick children have had roses named after them and many charities have benefited from the naming of roses.

May I end with the hope that many will be encouraged to give this lovely book to family and friends and that more people will wear roses in their buttonholes as I have been doing for more than 30 years worldwide and by so doing have made many new rose loving friends.

9

Spirit of the Rose

David Lloyd

What a fantastic journey! This part of it began following the launch of *Floramondi*, the book published to celebrate the 7th World Flower Show held in Glasgow 2002. I knew then that it would be a greatly missed opportunity to lose the momentum, and many friends were asking 'What next?!' Another book – of course! But what should the subject be? The overall content was obvious, but where was the focus to lie?

To the surprise of some I am sure, I settled on 'The Rose'. Little did I realise what I had begun. But one of the first people to react was Annie Beagent whose immediate belief in the credibility of the concept I outlined was more than encouraging. 'Spirit of the Rose' was born! Annie has since been the mainstay during the more difficult moments; bad weather does not help and our British climate is hardly consistent. But her infectious enthusiasm, good humour and overall desire to ensure the success of the project, have been priceless assets. Her sensitive styling and intuitive interpretations have enhanced many of the images and her printing skills are revealed in the exhibitions accompanying the book.

We soon realised that the scale of the subject was so massive that various criteria would have to be established. 'You will only have up to two weeks to shoot it,' I was told. Wrong? It has taken us two years. Who would have believed that the front cover would be shot in February 2004 using the brand new range of Cut Flower English Roses, bred and grown by David Austin Roses? Although it is true that lovely Dorothy in Tipperary often has her beloved Queen Elizabeth roses in her garden at Christmas! Rosebie Morton's growing fields were visited in late autumn, producing a rich tapestry of roses and autumn leaves.

With the obvious appeal of the 'English rose', we decided to concentrate solely on the United Kingdom for our inspiration. This did mean there would necessarily be some obvious omissions for who could ignore Empress Josephine or Pierre-Joseph Redouté when speaking of the rose? These, and many other worldwide rose stories will be featured and acknowledged in the future!

It is just not possible to include everyone and every facet of the rose story in one book. Neither an encyclopaedia nor a textbook, *Spirit of the Rose* is

perceived as a gift, as indeed is the rose itself. What is more uplifting than the sight and scent of a single rose or a magnificent display either in the garden or home? Without a doubt roses are always in fashion. Many a young man still today rushes out to buy his loved one a bouquet of red roses. Indeed, over one million blooms per day pass through Europe's flower markets on Valentine's Day and Mother's Day, many from as far afield as Africa and South America.

As a still-life photographer I have drawn on personal experience to capture the beauty of the one flower I find so endlessly fascinating. One of my inspirations has been Rachel Ruysch (1664-1750), the Dutch flower painter, and I trace my interest in fine art back to childhood visits to The Walker Art Gallery in Liverpool. As with so many who love the rose, I too was captivated by the roses that flourished in my grandparents' gardens.

One fascinating co-incidence on this voyage of floral adventure was being taken to the Rose Theatre on London's South Bank. This has proved to be such a strong link with our subject that a percentage of the profits from this book will go to the Rose Theatre Trust at which venue it is believed Shakespeare first performed.

I am in awe at the amount of knowledge and experience there is in the world of roses. I can only thank all those who have shared their passion with open hearts and generosity. Who could not be charmed by the wealth of information in *The Gardener's Chapbook* edited by EHM Cox or *A Book about Roses* by Dean Reynolds Hole, a true classic, both gifts from a friend caught up in the excitement of the project. I have had the privilege of working with a wonderful team of contributors and friends offering inspiration, support and enthusiasm along the way. I thank you all.

I am no gardener or rosarian but I do have a deep and abiding passion for this beautiful flower, in all its guises. I hope I have gone some way in doing her justice. I give you this extract from a Foreword to the letters of Samuel Reynolds Hole by G A Dewar, who writes: '"*A Book about Roses*" is truly a picture of Hole's disposition. Sun and Breeze play through it as they played through him. It sparkles with a joy quite infectious. One dips into it over and over again to find poesy and pun and practice so winningly blent'. I hope *Spirit of the Rose* can do a little of the same.

The Blossom of Aphrodite

Edna Johnson

There is no other flower that has entwined itself into the human imagination as the rose, for a rose is far more than just a rose, it is the 'Queen of Flowers' and nature's supreme creation. Even in its wild state it was already inspiring poets not only for the beauty of its blossom but the intoxication of its scent and it has given rise to countless tributes in all languages. It is a symbol of beauty and love, an expression of poets who seem to have a particular passion for roses, the emblem of kings and Paradise, Christian Mysticism, an ingredient of medicine and an embellishment of buildings and coins. Omar Khayyam 1048-1131 the Persian poet, addressing the vendor of roses cried: 'Why doest thou sell the rose for silver, for what more precious than the rose canst buy?'

The rose became a symbol of joy; petals were strewn before conquerors. The word 'rose' is almost a synonym for 'flower' and is used in many flower names such as Christmas Rose, *Helleborus niger*, Rose of Sharon, *Hypericum*, Tuberose, *Polianthes tuberosa*, by European translators unaware of botanical nomenclature, but gave those familiar names to flowers that could not possibly have been roses.

Fossil specimens 35 million years old have been found in Montana and Oregon, North America. This most ancient of plants was established on earth long before man. Found in monastery gardens after the Dark Age, in the Middle Ages there was a veritable cult of the rose.

It is fascinating to trace the influence that the rose had on Art. In the Romanesque period, a master builder would use rosettes on buildings. The rose window, colourful and mysterious was the 'Eye of God'. Rose windows were to be found in every important cathedral in France, Germany and England. Gloucester and Norwich show how master builders worked rose bush patterns into designs for arches. This is particularly clear in the unforgettable rose pillar at York Cathedral. All these works of art indicate how powerful was the impact of the oriental rose in the Middle Ages. For artists and for all who appreciated this work it must have been a symbol of beauty that demanded to be made into an immortal image, for in those days the rose still held a mystic significance of pentagram and was embodied in beauty, love and happiness.

The oldest picture of the flower is on the Minoan Fresco and an Egyptian tomb painting. Homer tells us that there were roses on the shield of Achilles and on the helmet of Hector. To Cleopatra, use of the flower became a craze at the banquets she gave for Mark Antony when the Queen was reputed to have ordered the floor to be covered 18" deep in roses petals. Romans scattered rose petals everywhere and bedecked guests with garlands of roses. They made rose wine, rose puddings and dropped petals in wine to prevent, or at least delay, drunkenness.

By the 13th Century the rose had become one of the most important symbols of the Holy Trinity, the Holy Joy of redeemed souls in paradise. Painters of all schools depicted Mary in rose gardens or crowned with roses. Many legends however tell of the miraculous creation of the Roman Catholic rosary when the prayers of a pious monk were changed into roses as they fell from his lips. The Pope gives a golden rose annually to an important person in the Church or City. The metal roses awarded first in 1049 were blessed on Rose Sunday or Laetare Sunday, 4th Sunday of Lent.

Roses must have embodied the solace and peace sought by the Empress Josephine as, alone in the rose garden at Malmaison, she left forever the gaiety and splendour of life with Napoleon. In her garden she tried to recreate a paradise of orchids, lilies and above all roses. In doing so she played an important role in the development of the modern rose. Botanists from all over the world would send roses to the Empress at Malmaison. Fortunately for future generations many of the superb roses in her collection were painted by Redouté. If paradise is a garden of the immortal, Redouté may be said to have immortalised some of the loveliest roses in the Empress's garden.

We like to think that there was something particularly English about the rose as it was adopted as our national emblem. The red rose of York and the white rose of Lancaster were chosen as emblems of those rival Houses until the two families were finally united in the reign of Henry VII. Roses were used as coronets of English Dukes and Marquesses, on the insignia of the Order of the Garter and the Order of Bath, on the seal of Scotland and on many coins.

From the beginning man has associated the rose with love and the magic of love. Poets throughout the world have made the rose a symbol of perfection and beauty, especially the beauty of women. The medieval epic 'Roman de la Rose', a tale of a young man's quest for the rosebud with which he had fallen in love, is probably the most famous of rose poems.

Gertrude Stein 1874-1946 wrote 'A Rose is a Rose is a Rose'. What an understatement! For a rose is far more than just a rose, it is the Queen of Flowers, a symbol of beauty and love, an expression of Christian Mysticism, an emblem of Kings and of Paradise, an ingredient of medicine and magic. Roses are miracles of colour, of form, of scent, of beauty – no other flower has created so much passion and joy as the blossom of Aphrodite, the Queen of flowers.

The Rose – What it means to us

Ian & Barbara Pollard at Abbey House Gardens

When looking into the history of our five-acre garden site in Malmesbury for information to which we might allude in our plans to open to the public by the Millennium, Ian was particularly impressed by what he had learned of the history and cultivation of roses. In the world of plants and flowers what other species has been in cultivation for over 3000 years, varies so widely in growth habit and in size of bloom, can flower for up to six months, be evergreen or deciduous, can live for years, withstands drought, produces fruits in amazing hues, has the widest variety of colour in blooms, texture, leaf forms and possesses the most exquisite perfumes known to man? We had to plant roses.

The history of roses is totally absorbing. In their book, The Quest for the Rose, *Roger Phillips & Martyn Rix chart the plant's existence from 35 million years ago. Their description of the Romans' love and use of roses tells of their 'production' having been a considerable industry at that time. Roses were symbols of life, death, courage, beauty, purity, and revelry. Roses were depicted on murals, wreaths adorned with roses were worn by gods and by emperors who might also shower petals on their guests at banquets. Sufficient, so we are told, to suffocate some at the feasts prepared for Heliogabalus in AD204-224. Roses perfumed the air, were laid on pillows, stuffed into cushions and eaten in a variety of dishes. Small wonder that the early Christian church in England tried to disassociate itself from these pagan, Roman connections when they banned the rose from cultivation for several centuries. Roses continued to grow in Monastery gardens however, where they flourished under the care of monks eager to reap essential oils for remedies, culinary purposes and of course for perfumery: uses we still have today. Long ago, within the Christian church, the rose came to symbolise the Virgin Mary and thus the rose returned to favour.

How fitting then to bring roses back to a garden where they had undoubtedly been cultivated during the time of obscurity; our grounds having formerly belonged to the Benedictine Monastery established on Malmesbury's ancient hill in the 7th century AD.

The opportunities for development of a rose garden here at Abbey House Gardens were wonderful. When we arrived in 1994, half the garden's five acres had been completely neglected over the previous 20 years but the soil was still in good order as it had been worked for centuries. With the Millennium looming we could not resist the urge to plant 2000 different roses within an overall planting scheme that is now home to 10,000 trees, shrubs and flowering plants.

Finding 2000 different roses was not as easy as you might think. Although thousands more are bred, (6000 in the United States alone), few breeders keep a large variety in stock for obvious reasons. Once we reached 1200 the pressure was on. However we received help from generous-spirited and knowledgeable rosarians who put us in touch with smaller breeders. At this point we needed to be careful of synonyms to avoid duplicating varieties already established but gradually we found the numbers we wanted, and more. Our plan was to celebrate the shrub's diversity.

As the well-known English garden designer, Gertrude Jekyll observed:

'We have only to place {rambling roses} well and show them how to go, to lead and persuade them just at the beginning. In two years' time they will understand what is wanted, and will gladly do it of themselves in many ways of their own – ways much better than any that we could possibly have devised.'

Today I marvel at *R*. 'Pheasant' with its vigorous profusion of small pink flowers. We cultivate this as a weeping standard as well as for groundcover. The climber 'Dublin Bay' with its perfectly formed blooms and gorgeous red flowers are complemented with beautiful mid-green foliage. *R*. 'Sally Holmes' is a favourite of Ian's. He describes this strong-growing shrub as a cream bouquet growing on a stem. I love the rambler 'Rose-Marie Viaud' for its luminous colour, the lavender side of pink, which conveys itself across an acre of garden to greet your eyes in early evening. It is fantastic.

We begin the mammoth task of deadheading in late June (by the end of the season we will have removed half a million heads) but this is an essential task to keep up the display until the first frosts appear.

Can I find a word aptly to describe the response of one's senses to the perfume and colour you see before you in the first flushes of June and July? – 'WOW' (and that's just what Alan Titchmarsh said when he first set eyes on our garden paradise!).

Won't you come into the garden?
I would like my roses to see you.

Richard Brinsley Sheridan

Shakespeare and the Rose

Susannah York

Roses in my life.

I well remember standing on tiptoes to stick my nose into a bloom in my grandmother's garden, inhaling the sweet perfume and saying, before I overbalanced, 'I could go to Heaven smelling that smell'. 'You don't know how lucky you are Susie!' Granny snapped as she picked me up, for poor Granny had lost her sense of smell.

We all know that roses are ephemeral, that is part of their beauty. As our mother explained, 'Nothing lasts for ever!' However, although roses in plant form may not have a long life, the love of a rose keeps returning in my life, through my love of Shakespeare and clearly, his works are everlasting.

Growing up on the west coast of Scotland, I became entranced when, on a day too wet to go rambling or riding, some of Shakespeare's marvellous characters walked out of the Indian-paper pages of the dark green, leather-bound volumes borrowed from the bookshelves of my actor-manqué stepfather. Of course we read Shakespeare at school too. In the big classrooms we read him aloud (the way to love him, I believe, savouring the words in our strong accents, puzzling over meanings, rejoicing when we understood and, gender-regardless, became his people: Juliet, Rosalind, Hamlet, Puck, Cleopatra, Mercutio, Beatrice, they took me by storm. There was Hamlet again for A-level. Then, at RADA Shakespeare jostled along with Beckett, Coward, Osborne, Congreve, Chekov and Ibsen – and we all became more of his people as we struggled with practice skirts', diction, breath control, iambic pentameters and for that elusive magical quality; stillness.

For a while, I lost him. I worked on plays, films, television all over the world, yet with almost no classical acting until, a few years ago in Connecticut, I was in a production of Hamlet set between a duck-pond and a railway-line when the Danish Prince's tragedy unfolded to the rattle of family picnics on the grass, the squeals of children at Star Wars in the wings and the thunder of trains, those incredibly long ones. Every quarter of an hour we had to freeze mid-soliloquy for four minutes. The relentless chirrup of crickets rose to a crescendo as stars came out and our audience melted in gaggles away.

But I was hooked once more. Back in England I joined the Royal Shakespeare Company and fell in love all over again. When calls came a couple of years ago to drop the Man of the Millenium from the state-school curriculum, I was off on my quest to play some of the women I had as yet not had the chance to characterise, to revel again in the language and above all, if I could, to lift the curtain on the perceived difficulties which for so many people, from their school days perhaps, seems to shroud Shakespeare. I wanted to show what I had learned: how accessible he becomes as soon as you start to speak him, that he is forever because he is so now. With their griefs and joys, relationships and predicaments, his characters renew themselves, like roses. And so I devised my show The Loves of Shakespeare's Women, playing it in theatres, universities and schools around the United Kingdom, as well as in Hungary, Georgia, Australia, the Far East, and with plans to visit Poland, the States and South America in 2004 and, who knows where else.

On Valentine's Day I played Shakespeare's women at the Rose Theatre, where, before the move to the Globe Theatre just a few steps away on The South Bank of London, the plays of both Shakespeare and Marlowe had been performed. It was an awesome feeling to be the first actor in 400 years to perform Shakespearean characters on that site; and to be the first actress ever! I remember feeling with a particular keenness, that my life so far has been a long, bumpy, exciting journey from Shakespeare and back to him again; and that night at the Rose, this sonnet, a favourite of mine with which I closed the show, seemed to have an extra relevance:

O, never say that I was false of heart,
Though absence seem'd my flame to qualify.
As easy might I from myself depart
As from my soul, which in thy breast doth lie:
This is my home of love: if I have ranged,
Like him that travels, I return again,
Just to the time, not with the time exchanged,
So that myself bring water for my stain.
Never believe: though in my nature reign'd
All frailties that besiege all kinds of blood,
That it could so preposterously be stain'd,
To leave for nothing all thy sum of good;
For nothing this wide universe I call,
Save thou, my Rose, in it thou art my all.

CIX; Sonnet: by William Shakespeare

The Rose and Shakespeare

The seasons alter: hoary-headed frosts
Fall in the fresh lap of the crimson rose.

A Midsummer Night's Dream

Pluck a red rose from off this thorn with me.

Somerset. Henry VI Part I

From off this briar pluck a white rose with me.

Plantaganet. Henry VI

Say that she frown; I'll say she looks as clear
As morning roses newly wash'd with dew.

Romeo & Juliet

Then, for the truth and plainness of the case,
I pluck this pale and maiden blossom here
Giving my verdict on the white rose side.

King Henry VI

But earthlier happy is the rose distilled,
Than that which withering on the virgin thorn
Grows, lives, and dies, in single blessedness

A Midsummer Night's Dream

'Think of me. God willing'

Tony Toller

The Rose Theatre, Bankside

When the site of the Rose Theatre on Bankside was first discovered in 1989, it yielded up a treasure-trove of interesting objects. These included jewellery, leatherwork, coins, tokens, eating utensils, and fragments of the boxes used to collect the entrance money. Not least among these treasures was a gold ring engraved with a heart and two arrows, bearing the inscription 'PENCES POVR MOYE D(eus) V(ult)' in archaic French meaning 'THINK OF ME. God Willing'. Unearthed after 400 years or more, it was still in beautiful condition.

Theories about this ring abound. To whom did it belong? Was it the property of a groundling standing in the yard, or of an 'uppermost' person seated in the gallery? Did it belong to Shakespeare or Marlowe? Was it an engagement ring? – Or some other love token? An eternity ring perhaps? Whatever the truth, it would make an intriguing story.

A romantic story, perhaps, linked to the exciting times in which it took place: the loss of the ring, the search for it, the heartache, the people involved. And the final, sad realisation that it was lost forever. Indeed it would be a story worthy of the first Elizabethan theatre to be built on Bankside, the theatre where the ring was found over four hundred years later. It's a story simply waiting to be written.

The Rose was the first theatre to be built on Bankside by one Philip Henslowe in 1587. Henslowe was born in Lindfield, Sussex, around 1550, and by 1577 was living in Southwark, not far from the site that was to become home to the Rose. He had been apprenticed to a dyer, and after his master's death, married his rich widow – a story as intriguing as the story of the ring! With his wife's money, Henslowe acquired a good deal of property on Bankside, including inns, lodging houses and brothels – or 'stews', as they were known. This marriage also gained him a stepdaughter, Joan Woodward, who, five years after the Rose was built, married a famous actor of the day, Edward Alleyn. Henslowe, ever the shrewd businessman, made his son-in-law a business partner and together they were responsible for the success of the Rose.

In 1587 the first stage of building would have been for Henslowe and the carpenter, John Griggs, to survey the ground and lay out the theatre plan – a fourteen-sided polygon, some 22 metres in diameter. The inner and outer walls of the main structure were set 3.5 metres apart. With the foundations in place, a few courses of bricks were put in to support the main timber-framed structure, which was filled in with wattle and plaster and roofed with thatch. Galleries contained seating, while 'groundlings' stood in the open yard below. The front of the stage projected well into this yard and the area behind it served as the actors' dressing and props room.

The Rose was only the fifth purpose-built theatre in London, in an area already rich in leisure attractions, a number of which were owned by Henslowe. Little is known about the Rose before Edward Alleyn became associated with its fortunes in 1592. After that date much more information came to light through documents belonging to Henslowe and Alleyn. Henslowe himself began to keep a Diary in 1592. More like an account book, it gives important details about the quite extensive alterations carried out at the Rose in that year. The bays in the northern part of the building were shifted outwards so as to enlarge it. The stage was moved back and re-angled a little off-centre. This allowed for a full bay opening of about nine feet in the centre of the rear of the stage. Had it been positioned dead centre, there would have been a twelve inch square oak post right in the middle of the main section of the frons scenae. Moving it round a bit would have created ample space, in one full bay of the fourteen sides creating a wide opening or 'discovery space'. Such a broad opening, with a smaller door on each flanking side, would have been necessary for the famous entry of Tamburlaine in his chariot pulled by four kings. The work also included the resurfacing of the yard with a mixture of compacted cinder and hazelnut shells. These shells seem to have been the by-product of a local soap making industry and not, as was first thought in 1989, the Elizabethan equivalent of popcorn!

The Diary also lists the plays subsequently put on at the Rose and the type of audiences they attracted. The hugely popular repertory included Shakespeare's Titus Andronicus and Henry VI Part 1, Marlowe's Doctor Faustus, The Jew of Malta and Tamburlaine the Great, and Kyd's Spanish Tragedy. There are also lists of the stage properties and the costumes worn for some of these productions. The Diary, together with the other documents, make up a uniquely rich source for studying the Elizabethan stage, which has made it possible to establish the history of the Rose in far greater detail than that of any other contemporary playhouse.

The spirit of the Rose captivates everyone who today visits the site to be greeted by the ghosts that are said to dwell there. For the archaeologists there is still much for the site to yield up. There are treasures still to be found, questions to be answered, and so much more to learn. God willing.

29

Garland of Roses

William Shakespeare

Live with me and be my love
And we will all the pleasures prove
That hills and valleys, dales and fields
And all the craggy mountains yield,

There we will sit upon the rocks,
And see the shepherds feed their flocks,
By shallow rivers, by whose falls
Melodious birds sing madrigals

There will I make thee a bed of roses
With a thousand fragrant posies.
A cap of flowers and a kirtle
Embroidered all with leaves of myrtle

A belt of straw and ivy buds,
With coral clasps and amber studs:
And if these pleasures may thee move,
Then live with me and be my love.

Love's Answer
If that the world and love were young,
And truth in every shepherd's tongue,
These pretty pleasures might me move
To live with thee and be thy love.

Shakespeare: Love's Labours Lost

A Midsummer Night's Dream

William Shakespeare

I know a bank whereon the wild thyme blows,
Where oxlips and the nodding violet grows
Quite over-canopied with luscious woodbine,
With sweet musk-roses, and with eglantine.

William Shakespeare

A Dark Lady at Gawsworth

Elizabeth Richards

It has been said that to see the county of Cheshire you must see Gawsworth. The ancient village lies two miles to the south of Macclesfield where the Cheshire plain meets the foothills of the Pennines. There are few more satisfying sights than the black and white half-timbered Hall with its manicured lawns reflected in the lake. In medieaval times the village consisted only of the Hall, the Church, Rectory and a handful of cottages lying within easy walking distance of the heart of the parish.

In 1070, the De Orrebys were the first recorded family to live in the original manor house adjacent to the Norman chapel. Later, in the 14th century they married into the Fitton family and, as a result of this union, Gawsworth prospered and grew into the village we know today. In the second half of the 15th century, the old wooden manor house was replaced by the present Hall; the chapel being replaced by the splendid perpendicular church in 1480. Finally, in 1500 the Fittons completed the magnificent rectory. This group of buildings still meets the visitors' gaze as they turn the corner in Church Lane. It is as though time has been compressed over five hundred years, Patron and Priest still living side by side with the Church as central feature.

The Hall was home to the Fittons for two hundred and fifty years. The family gradually grew in stature with the passing of time; warriors, peacemakers, landowners of great wealth, their influence spread throughout the county. However, it was during the reign of Elizabeth I that tragedy and triumph walked hand in hand for Sir Edward Fitton and his family. Young Mary found herself in the royal court as a Maid of Honour to the Queen. The story goes that she met Shakespeare at this time and they fell in love, Shakespeare writing his sonnets to the Dark Lady i.e. Mary. But the path of true love is never simple or straightforward: Mary forsook Shakespeare for the Earl of Pembroke. The outcome was a stillborn child, Pembroke imprisoned in the notorious Fleet prison, and Mary banished to Gawsworth while Shakespeare's sonnets turned from pure love to disappointment and dismay. Whether you believe this story or not, theirs was the generation that landscaped the whole of the Gawsworth area to make it fit for a visit from the Queen, who of course, never came. This great garden scheme involved moving the village, enlarging the lakes, and building the wall surrounding the inner garden that stretches for nearly a mile. Such was its scale and expense that the family finances never recovered.

The death of Mary's brother, yet another Sir Edward Fitton and the first baronet, led to more controversy. With no male heirs, the estate should have passed to the Irish Fittons but instead Sir Edward named his favourite nephew, Charles Gerrard. The dispute over the estate known as the 'Great Cheshire Will Case' was mentioned in Samuel Pepys' Diaries and rumbled on for the whole of the Civil War, only to be resolved at the Restoration of Charles II. Both Sir Edward Fitton and Charles Gerrard fought for the Royalist cause, the latter gaining the rank of Major General in the King's army. Later centuries include the infamous duel between Lord Mohun and the Duke of Hamilton in 1712 over the estate when both combatants perished. Then came the peaceful tenure of the Stanhope family, Earls of Harrington, who for two hundred years regarded Gawsworth as just one property amongst the many they owned throughout the country. The whole estate was sold in 1921 bringing us to modern times.

Now the Richards family live in this fascinating old house, and as times change they have adapted the Hall to cope with present day financial pressures whilst still preserving the atmosphere of old. House opening, the much loved open air theatre, car rallies, weddings and even craft fairs sit easily within the precincts, whilst the house looks at its loveliest for Barry Grey's amazing displays of flowers at Christmas. Gawsworth is enjoying a second golden age of love and admiration.

Floreat Aula

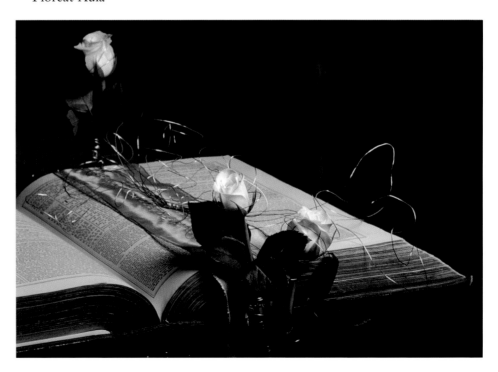

The Medicinal Rose

Annie Beagent

Use of the rose for medicinal purposes is not new nor is it specific to one area. Preparations using the rose, feature in many cultures including traditional Indian, Egyptian, Chinese, and Arabian. In ancient Persia roses were used in religious ceremonies and were considered a cure for both internal and external ailments. Rose oil was used as a base to prepare balms of all kinds, and rosewater almost considered a panacea, a cure all.

The rose also held a prominent place in Western medicine. In the fourth century BC Hippocrates wrote of a perfumed rose oil prepared for Anatolia by macerating fresh roses in olive oil. He prescribed rose medicaments for use in gynaecological conditions. In the first century AD, Dioscorides compiled *Materia Medica*.

The work explored Greek and Egyptian herbal lore and was referred to well into the seventeenth century.

A contemporary of Dioscorides, Pliny the Elder, listed 32 conditions that could benefit from treatment incorporating the rose. Even in AD 76, the rose was recognised as a plant that could be prepared as a medicine to treat inflammations, aches, pains, abrasions and sleeplessness. Pliny also wrote of how wealthy Romans filled their baths with rose petals to keep the body young. There was also a method described to cure a hangover!

During the Middle Ages the Gallic Rose was grown in monastery gardens; their dried petals often available from the apothecary, thus the name 'The Apothecary Rose', which continued to play a part in history and literature.

In the 16th Century, John Gerard, (1545-1612) an Elizabethan physician, published the Historie of Plants. Gerard did not always acknowledge the source of his observations. Plagiarism was rife and his works open to interpretation. It may be possible that his works provoked heated discourse between the academic and the practitioner. However, it cannot be said of now, or of then, that the rose was dismissed as a major player in the history of the plant world. Gerard hailed the virtues of the rose for its restorative properties, its ability to refresh the spirit and to strengthen the heart. He also suggested that its flavour enhanced food, hot and cold and that the petals and leaves could be preserved in sugar to be used to make sugar roses and conserve.

Nicholas Culpeper (1616-1654) the British herbalist and astrologer regarded the rose highly and wrote of it more than any other plant or herb.

During the 18th Century, traditional remedies in the Western World were replaced by chemistry. Drugs were created using synthetic substitutes – extract of lead appearing in many compounds! The rose was relegated to a flower possessing a good scent valuable in the manufacture of perfume. Many other countries steeped in tradition however, continued to grow and use the rose using recipes handed down throughout history.

During the Second World War, when supplies of food and medicines were in short supply, the rose regained an important position in the West and was regarded as one of the best providers of vitamin C. It was also used to cleanse the digestive system and flowers picked to produce home-made perfumes and rosewater.

The rose, some species more than others, has now been scientifically researched in many countries. Findings prove that it does indeed possess a number of medicinal qualities and that ancient recipes, correctly administered, can offer an alternative to medicines produced scientifically using chemistry. Perhaps it shows that 'old wives tales' have a sound base and need not always be disregarded!

The Christmas Rose

Know ye the flower that just now blows,
In the middle of winter – the Christmas Rose?
A plant, indeed, of the Crowsfoot kind,
Not really a Rose – but never mind,
It blooms out o'doors in the garden bed,
Its petals are white with a tinct of red.
Though it lacketh perfume to regale the nose,
To the eyes right fair is the Christmas Rose.
A fiddlestick's end for the frost and snows;
Sing hey, sing ho, for the Christmas Rose.

Your Christmas Rose is a lovely flower,
But a herb with a root of marvellous power,
Helleborus niger – the Hellebore,
Which the leeches, both Latin and Greek, of yore
In high repute as a remedy had,
Withal to physic the crazed and mad,
So lunatics, as the story goes,
They sent to the Isle of the Christmas Rose.
A fiddlestick's end for the frost and snows;
Sing hey, sing ho, for the Christmas Rose.

Anon

Roses in Symbolism and Art

Michael Bowyer

Throughout history, surely no flower has ever been more loved or more inbued with meaning than the rose. From ancient times the rose has decorated buildings, rooms and tables and adorned the very person of those living in far off times. At a splendid Alexandrian banquet given by Cleopatra in honour of Julius Caesar, all the guests were crowned with roses. She later repeated the act for Mark Antony, this time strewing the floor ankle deep in rose petals.

Roman emperors were also noted for their extravagance with roses. Nero, who decreed that petals should be strewn in front of him as he walked on the beach near Naples, is credited as the first to shower his guests with rose petals cascading from the specially built panels in the ceiling of his villa. This act was repeated to excess by Heliogabalus some one hundred and fifty years later when three canopy loads, which must have initially delighted his guests, eventually suffocated them.

In Rome, at the spring festival of Ludi Florales, maidens would dance through the streets holding flower-filled scarves; doubtless roses would have been included. Pliny mentions twelve varieties of roses growing at this time, many of them cultivated in Egypt and shipped twice monthly to Ostia, the port of Rome.

The legal term *sub rosa* dates from this period when a bunch of white roses hung from the ceiling denoted that secrecy was to be observed.

It is at this time we find evidence of roses being arranged with other flowers, for in Hadrian's villa near Tivoli was the famous mosaic of a basket of flowers, now preserved in the Vatican Museum.

The Greeks too had decorative uses for rose petals. Braided petals were placed around the rims of drinking glasses and, filled with wine, the vessels even had rose petals floating on the top. At this time a man could receive nothing more erotic than the wilted wreath of roses that had, the evening before, adorned the head of the object of his desire, delivered with added apples from which she had taken a bite.

It was to be many years before floral decoration again became important in the west.

The artists of the Italian Renaissance included arrangements of flowers in their paintings of religious subjects. However, it must be said that in these paintings the lily and the iris often took precedence over the rose. Filled with religious symbolism each painted flower was endowed with meaning: violets for humility, the daisy for innocence, an orange lily for the Christ Child, the rose representing the Virgin Mary as Queen of Heaven.

During the seventeenth century in Holland too, the rose was eclipsed, this time by the tulip. Today we love to recreate those Dutch Flemish flower pieces originally painted by van Huysum, de Heem, Walscapelle and Rachel Ruysch, remembering, of course, that the originals did not exist but were created in the studio from botanical drawings sketched in the gardens of wealthy patrons where new plants from across the globe were being amassed, delighting their owners on their first flowering.

In these paintings the rose often depicted the transience of life, especially when the petals had fallen gracefully on to the marble base, or when the leaves showed distinct signs of insect damage.

Many such paintings, particularly those by Jan Breugel, showed a hierarchy of flowers, at the top of the floral design are those associated with the holy family: the lily and iris in particular. Just above the rim of the vase are wild or humble flowers, whilst roses are included in the central band of noble flowers along with carnations and peonies.

Roses adorn much of the exquisite china produced at the Sévrès factory in eighteenth century France. Originally situated at Vincennes, in 1750 Madame de Pompadour thrilled the King and her guests at a winter reception with banks of hothouse flowers, including roses, all made from china. So impressed was Louis XV that he bought up the factory and moved it to Sévrès where it produced wares decorated with the soft red 'Pompadour' rose. This rococo period with its 'S' and 'C' curves has long inspired flower arrangers, along with portraits of court favourites wearing beautiful silk gowns garlanded with (probably fake) roses, the sitter adorned with corsages at the neck, shoulder and wrist with flowers entwined in the hair.

One who bridges French revolutionary turmoil is Pierre-Joseph Redouté. Originally employed by Marie-Antoinette this remarkable rose painter subsequently became patented artist to the Empress Josephine immortalising the roses growing in her Malmaison garden.

We have to thank Lady Mary Wortley Montague for introducing 'the language of flowers' to Victorian society. Making up bouquets which portrayed the desires of the sender kept young Victorian men and women engrossed for hours as meanings behind each flower contained in the bunch was sought with the help of specially published books. These bunches inevitably contained a rose.

Roses were also included in the first prize-winning design in the first ever flower arranging competition held in 1861 at the Royal Horticultural Society`s new garden at South Kensington. The fashion for dining á la russe had become

popular, leaving large areas of the dining table free for decoration. Prizes were offered for the best three groups of fruit and flowers for the decoration of the dinner table. First prize went to Thomas March – yes, a man! – although it was rumoured that his sisters actually did the arranging. Roses with forget-me-nots, pansies, lily of the valley and ferns were held aloft on slender glass columns.

At the beginning of the twentieth century decorating with roses fell into two distinct camps. Whilst the Edwardians loved to arrange bowls of only one type of flower and usually only in one colour, perhaps with some added gypsophila, the Art Nouveau movement however, liked to mix their flower kinds, favouring those with sinuous stems and drooping heads such as bluebells and honeysuckle. The great Glasgow designer Charles Rennie Mackintosh stylized the rose, stencilling it on to walls and fabrics and working it into the stained glass doors of the Willow Tea Rooms in Glasgow. At the Turin exhibition in 1902 he and his wife, Margaret, produced an exhibit entitled 'The Rose Boudoir'.

In Great Britain, after the Second World War, a new movement began in Dorchester by Mary Pope. Enthusiasm spread rapidly throughout the country, bringing colour and excitement to the drab post-war years. These were the flower clubs, open to those with gardens small and large, which became popular,

as flowers were one of the few things not rationed in those days. In 1959, under the auspices of the RHS, these groups came together to form the National Association of Flower Arrangement Societies. A life vice-president of the society is Julia Clements OBE VMH, referred to today as the high priestess of flower arranging. Julia, who travelled the country, and the world, setting up new groups wherever she lectured, is fortunate in having three roses named after her: R. 'Julia Clements', 'Lady Seton' and 'Julia'. The latter is the most widely grown, being a subtle parchment shade beloved by flower arrangers.

Bill LeGrice Roses, which Company specialises in off-beat coloured roses has also bred others connected with the flower arranging movement. A former president R. 'Iris Webb' is a brown/gold , whilst R. 'Jocelyn', named after Jocelyn Steward (the first chairman of NAFAS) is brown and R. 'Mary Pope' a rich magenta.

Visit any flower show today and admire the beautiful floral designs created for exhibition or competition, chances are that many will contain roses seeking to portray love, luxury and beauty. Throughout the generations roses have been arranged with love in vases, bowls, posies and bunches and, for centuries have decorated major events and festivals. Where would the flower arranger be without the rose; where would the rose be without the flower arranger?

Sudeley Castle

Text by Spirit of the Rose

Sudeley, nestling within the Cotswolds, is steeped in history and royal connections spanning 1,000 years.

Queen Catherine Parr and Lady Jane Grey lived here. It is said that Henry VIII, en route to Berkeley Castle with Anne Boleyn, brought *Rosa mundi* to Sudeley, where it has been grown ever since. Queen Elizabeth I visited, King Charles I stayed and King George III also visited, even though by then the castle was a romantic ruin. In 1837 John and William Dent, Worcestershire glove makers, bought the Castle and began an ambitious restoration programme. The Castle is surrounded by ten smaller, beautiful gardens. The famous Queen's Garden, full of old-fashioned roses, herbs and topiary features, is flanked by two double yew hedges, planted by Emma, who was married to John Dent in 1847.

Now the home of Lord and Lady Ashcombe and the Dent-Brocklehurst family, the gardens are managed organically with a particular emphasis on conservation, sustainability, restoration and regeneration.

No one knows
Through what wild centuries
Roves back the rose.   Walter de la Mare

45

My Inspiration for English Roses

David Austin

While my passion for gardening and for plants started at a very early age, roses did not really feature until I became fascinated with the idea of breeding plants when I was about 18 or 19 years old. This came from my acquaintance with James Baker of Bakers Nurseries who introduced new varieties of Hardy Plants including Russell's Lupins, phloxes, delphiniums and many others. I cast around looking for plants to work on and 'improve', first trying my hand at grasses.

It was not until I read George Bunyard's book on Old Roses that I realised what wonderful plants roses could be. In the 1940s, Old Roses were out of favour and were fast being lost to cultivation. The emphasis was on Hybrid Teas that I did not particularly like and, really, were not very good plants. Rose breeders at that time concentrated mainly on the beauty of the flower and ignored, to my mind, crucial characters like fragrance, shape of plant and that rather indefinable character, charm. Many Old Roses have an abundance of these characteristics, although the one character they do lack (a rather dubious omission as very few plants have it) is repeat flowering. So I set about trying to introduce repeat flowering into the Old Roses without losing any of their beauty and charm.

I was also keen to keep the beautiful and very variable Old Rose shape of the flower. Many have the classically full flowers with well over 100 petals but then the petals are arranged in many different ways – rosette, quartered rosette, cupped, rounded (cabbage), recurved or pompon. Others may only have a few petals but are by no means less beautiful and indeed many regard them as more beautiful. One of the features of Old Rose blooms that never ceases to amaze and delight me is that of the distinct stages through which the blooms all go as they develop, mature and fade, each phase stunning in its beauty. I have always strived to incorporate these characteristics into my English Roses.

I first started breeding roses purely as a hobby, in 1945. It was the late Graham Thomas who introduced my first rose, Constance Spry, in 1961. This glorious rose has a wonderful fragrance but does not repeat flower. I continued crossing roses and by 1969 had my first group of six repeat flowering varieties that I called English Roses. They were the basis of my nursery, started that same year when I also offered the whole range of roses – both Old and New.

The popularity of English Roses was greatly enhanced by the introduction, in 1983, of *R.* 'Mary Rose' and 'Graham Thomas'. The latter especially caught the attention of gardeners with its rich yellow blooms. Since then I have introduced about 100 varieties, their qualities improving all the time as my breeding programme has become more refined and finances have allowed me to grow more seedlings, now about 250,000 each year. In the last few years, my aim has been to introduce disease-free English Roses, crucially without compromising their beauty, fragrance and charm.

I find roses endlessly fascinating, they are so variable in all their characteristics. There is a rose for just about every position in the garden and every climate in the world. There are roses that grow in very hot climates, others that survive some of the coldest weather in the Northern Hemisphere. Some are tiny plants a few centimetres tall, others are tens of metres tall. They will grow in deserts or in river plains flooded for six months of the year. Their flowers have petal counts of between four and two hundred and include every colour except true blue. They have an extraordinarily wide range of fragrances. There are very few genera that can boast so much variability.

One of the aspects I find particularly alluring is their fragrance. As far as I know roses are unique in the plant world for having such a wide range of quite different fragrances.

51

There are five basic types:

Old Rose –The classic rose fragrance, the one that you might expect all roses to smell of. It is this fragrance that is extracted in rose oil, a tiny drop of which enriches the best perfumes.

Tea Rose – A very different fragrance, reminiscent of a freshly opened packet of china tea, possibly somewhat of an acquired taste but then, much appreciated.

Musk – Unlike the other fragrances that come from the petals, musk originates from the stamens and wafts wonderfully on the air. It can resemble the true musk fragrance from deer but is also often strongly reminiscent of cloves.

Myrrh – Difficult to describe, possibly closest to the anis fragrance found in Sweet Cicely, Myrrhis odorata, hence the name. Very distinct and delicious.

Fruity – An enormously variable group in itself with just about every fruit you can find in the greengrocers, from the common apple, pear, strawberry, raspberry and citrus to the more unusual guava and lychee.

You will also find other fragrances that do not come neatly under the above headings – orris, heliotrope, nasturtium, green (as in cucumber), various flower blossoms – the list goes on.

To make the whole subject even more interesting many varieties will be a mixture of two or more different fragrances, the emphasis changing according to the weather at the time and some days before, the time of day and the stage of the flower. To quote an example, R. 'Golden Celebration' will start as tea scented, become more citrus, ending up as blackcurrant and along the way you will often get hints of strawberry and sauterne wine!

Added to the physical beauty of the rose is their fascinating history, how they have included themselves in our culture, in Europe, the Middle East, North Africa and Asia. You will find them in politics, religion, all the arts, as a symbol of love and loyalty and as an ingredient of perfumes, cosmetics and medicines.

Roses have played and still do play a unique role in our lives not just in our gardens but in our culture too. And I am sure they will continue to do so for a very long time.

53

Petals and Hips

Susie Edwards

Learning a new skill, particularly a delicate one, is always hard. I remember so well struggling with the art of attaching a fine rose wire to an individual rose petal, when I was participating in my course in floristry at the Constance Spry Flower School. I never believed I would ever be able to make this amazing open rose from the petals strewn in front of me. Like all tutors, ours had made it look so easy.

With perseverance and patience in vast quantities, petal by petal the pile grew until I was ready to put them all together and there it was, an overblown 'cabbage rose' made up from, if I remember correctly, six roses. It became a favourite piece of work and I used five of them as the centre of a delicate hand spray for the bride of the first wedding I did on my own. So it was lovely to be able to make one again for this book. They have dropped out of fashion as the demand for corsages has waned and I had not made one for years.

A couple of weeks after making it however, I opened a contemporary floral art magazine and saw the recipe and instructions to make a modern day Carmen rose using florists' cold glue! So much easier! And lighter on the lapel. The featured design was much bigger than my original corsage and had been created for a bride to carry as a bouquet. When I did my wedding bouquet I had made the largest roses I could using the wired method and had had to fashion five into a spray to achieve any size to the bouquet, but new materials and methods make it simple to make extra large individual roses. It just goes to show, though, there is nothing new in the world, just old ideas updated. This one has certainly stood the test of time.

There seems always to have been a flower in my hand. I dare say it will go on like that too. I have tried to give them up, sugar in my tea was easy, but flowers are engrained in every fibre of me. I ought to refine flower to 'part of plant' because leaves and fruits and grasses are as addictive! As a tiny child, afternoon country walks with my mother were opportunities to collect 'things'. We never came home without kindling for the fire, a primrose, a conker or stems of Quaking grass (briza), blackberries and particularly sprays of rose hips. Highly prized by wartime families, they were triumphantly delivered to my grandmother to be turned into rosehip syrup. It was fascinating to me that the best booty was always protected by vicious thorns. According to the illustration of rosehips in a treasured little book 'How to

Recognise Fruits and Berries' by Winifred E Bray (Price – three shillings and sixpence!), wild roses appear to be thornless! But the reality never put me off. I still have the book today, together with the Flower Fairies series and, as autumn begins to fall, I see all the drawings so clearly as I collect 'things' from the hedgerows. It used to grieve me that all the lovely red hips were put in the (blender) mincer; the destruction of those wonderful little beacons of autumn was so sad. I kept imagining the agony of the hip fairy and, as if to make a point, I always disliked rose-hip syrup! Somehow though it never changed my fondness for the hip's visible qualities.

It is miraculous that those soft sprays of delicate little pale pink flowers become such strong and striking stems of red and orange fruits. While they are in the immature stage, green and still, surrounded by foliage, they go almost unnoticed and then suddenly there they are studding the hedges and bushes with colour. It is such a difficult decision to make – long sprays for a piece of traditional work or close packed hips massed into a contemporary design. On my autumn forays into the countryside even just one or two added to a sprig of late heather, a yellowing fern frond and a stem of wood sage, put life into a little bunch for my kitchen table.

Recently I have come across a white multi headed rose that ends up with sprays of very tiny hips. It is being planted often in amenity schemes or on the banks of new road schemes Texturally these are so different from the Dog Rose hips, almost fussy they add a soft warmness within a design without making a huge statement.

There are many who, if reminded of the words 'rose hips' think of the fat Rugosa hips or those wonderful flagon-shaped ones full of character, but, to my chagrin, I have never had a large enough supply of either at any one time to be able to do anything spectacular with them, but wild roses always show themselves to me in volume and I am instantly inspired to use them.

I have a constant battle with the blackbird that 'owns' my garden. I gather enough hips to keep me going for a week or so only to find a bucket of bare twigs when I come to use them. He doesn't seem to mind whether they are ripe or not, it is just easier to have his food harvested for him than to fly over the road to the hedge. There are still hips hanging in that hedge until January, but bring one over to a bucket in the garden and its gone in a flash!

Arranging with hips can be dangerous, the thorns! – and difficult. As they ripen the joint between the fruit stem and main stem is easily broken so, when using them close packed to, say, cover a foam sphere, the stem you have left is both short and lacking in strength. Tedious as it might be, pre-made holes with a cocktail stick and the use of a small amount of cold florist glue saves the day, and your sanity. Used en masse to create an area of texture, hips take on a new

character, special visual value and are amazingly tactile. We underestimate the sense of touch and probably never even rate it as a true source of stimulus when designing with plant material for such a visual art, but for me the handling and feeling of plant material both during the making of a design and afterwards, add a great deal to the creation and to the final result.

Consider for a moment a hip – smooth, shiny, pointed, red – then a group of hips – craggy, rough, textured red. True to its name a very stylish part of the rose and currently very trendy too, ultra hip! I say hooray and I am not apologising for this.

Hip hip hooray!

'Rose Cottage'

David Lloyd

How could there be a book on The Rose without a Rose Cottage? Yet this Rose Cottage lies in the imagination! I do believe we all have a 'Rose Cottage' in our hearts and souls, a sanctuary, a spiritual home. But this one is in the mind and the writings of Dylan Thomas, in the classic *Under Milk Wood*.

Whether or not the characters and locations are inspired by Laugharne or his earlier sojourns in Cardiganshire is open to interpretation. What we do know is that Dylan adored and totally explored that beautiful county.

He often stayed and worked in Plas Gelli, Talsarn, a secluded country house. Indeed Dylan saw the Aeron Valley 'as the most precious place in the world.'

A tale from Plas Gelli, Talsarn. 'Interviews with Local people' from the book *'Dylan Thomas: A Farm Two Mansions and a Bungalow'* by David N. Thomas.

'Interview with Amanda Williams:

'Everybody staying at Gelli has heard or been disturbed by the ghost, Dylan as well.

'Another time, there was a lady – Gelli was empty now, and there was a rose at the front door – I don't think it's there now – a very pretty pink rose. It was at the side of the pillars and there was a lady, Miss Lewis, she said : "Oh, I'd love a piece of that rose", and she went over there one evening and she was cutting off the rose and a voice came from inside: "That's mine, leave that alone" and she had a hell of a fright, you know, she ran and she left everything as it was. And people were telling her, "You imagined it." "No," she said, "I heard a voice inside and there was nobody there." The house was empty then.'

63

The Rose Revived

Annie Beagent

The Rose Revived Inn sits on the north bank of the River Thames and over the bridge on the south bank stands another inn, The Maybush.

Newbridge, dates back to the 13th century and is reputed to be one of the oldest bridges in the country, separating the Inns, providing access to and from the market towns of Witney and Faringdon.

Although there is insufficient evidence to support this story totally, it is suggested that the bridge was built by the Monks of Deerhurst Priory, the art of building stone bridges in England having been lost with the departure of the Romans. By this time only monks possessed the necessary skills, including the building of pointed arches, which are a feature of Newbridge. The bridge is purported to have seen action in the Battle of Newbridge during the Civil War. Radcot Bridge, further along the Thames, built in 1200 by the Cistercian monks of St Mary, Citeaux in Normandy, had been severely damaged during the War of the Roses.

It is well documented that monks grew many plants for medicinal and culinary purposes, including roses, at this point in history. Apparently, the Inn was not originally called The Rose Revived nor was there any mention of a rose in the title until much later. However, one story suggests that a large rose bush grew in the gardens, which were devastated during a flood. As early as 1692 it was recorded that the river in the area of the bridge was subjected to serious flooding and, even today, The Maybush on the other bank is still blighted by this problem.

A photograph depicting the inn on the north bank in 1920, gives it the name of The Rose. It appears to be surrounded by water and the suggestion is that the rose bush was destroyed. A second photograph, dated 1923, shows the Inn with the name The Rose Revived!

Today the Inn is covered with roses in the summer months and its garden sits happily on the banks of the river Thames. Its secret is still hidden.

The Holy Rosary

Angela Parker

Pygmy Pinetum Garden Nursery

The Holy Rosary is not a rose garden or a garland, but Our Lady's Psalter. The Holy Rosary is the story of Our Lord as arranged by his Mother. The beads used to say Hail Marys (AVES), Our Fathers (Pater Nosters) and Glory Be's (Glorias), were originally said to have been made of carved roses; white Roses for the ten Aves and red Roses inserted for the Paters, symbolising the blood of Christ.

The rose has been revered by the Catholic Church and given Holy qualities. The Scripture in sacred history describes the journey from slavery to freedom, as 'the wilderness shall … rejoice and blossom as the rose'.

Mary, the Mother of God, is depicted as a rose:

Rosa mystica
There is no rose of such virtue
As is the rose that bore jesu: allelluia.
But of course Mary was the rose without thorns:
'But sweeter far is Mary's self
The rose without a thorn.'

Mary is recorded in the breviary of the rosary as saying: ' I have borne fruit like the rose '. The fourth Sunday of Lent is Rose Sunday and the Pope sends a golden rose, a piece of jewellery to the monarch of a Catholic state quoting: 'Take this rose from our hand which, however unworthy, occupies the place of god on earth, a rose…that most beautiful flower, which is the joy and crown of all the saints…'

When Mary appeared to St Bernadette in Lourdes she 'was clothed so modestly and without adornment (save for the exquisite detail of the two dawn-coloured roses at her feet).'

Mary revelled in roses, the Queen of the Angels, the Queen of Heaven wore crowns of roses, was surrounded by rose garlands and gave them away, in many wonderful works of art. She was the Madonna in a Garland of Roses, the Virgin of the Rose Garden, Madonna of the Rose Bower, and more.

One legend tells of a charming encounter between Our Lady and a youth saying his rosary:

'As each prayer left his lips,
She gathered it in her hand and it became a rosebud.
Of these flowers,
Our lady wove a crown and put it on her head.'

In Mary's month of May, we Catholic girls strewed our rose petals around the playground, walking before Mary's platform, dressed in white, white gloves and white veils with red polka dots (pater nosters, the rose red blood of Christ had become red felt polka dots) thinking less of Mary than of keeping in time with the prayer quietly chanted:

Sweet sac-(hand in the basket) ra-ment (kissing the petal)
We thee (turning around) adore (dropping the petal)
O make us love thee more and more
(Turning around, ready to begin again)!

This prayer is not addressed to her, but to her Son.

Collecting the roses required planning. While my aunt's rose petals were provided for her, we culled ours from neighbours' gardens!

Saying the Holy Rosary as we processed or, communally in church, sounded more like a quiet hum or chant as the words of the prayers faded into the background whilst we supposedly meditated on its Five Joyful, Five Sorrowful and Five Glorious Mysteries; The Holy Rosary, the story of the life of Christ, His birth and growing up, His death and His rising again, all expressed in Caryll Houselander's description of the woman of Bruges meditating over her rosary:

Her mind, like a velvet bee
Droning over a rose,
Gathers the honey of comfort
From the story of god.

From the streets of Bootle to the wonderful Royal Forest of Dean, I have now joined Mary as part of the Brethren of the Rose, a Rosarian, and I no longer need to cull them from any garden other than my own, at Pygmy Pinetum.

From Petals to Perfumes

John Bailey

An artisan perfumer's passion for the Queen of Flowers - The rose.

John Bailey's calling card describes him as an artisan perfumer, scent maker, scent historian, the appointed purveyor of the Royal National Rose Society's collection of classic rose perfumes. His passion stems from the first job on leaving school as an apprentice in the laboratories of a manufacturing chemist and druggist, learning the art and science of formulating and compounding aromatic plants for pills, potions and perfumes.

Since the dawn of history man has been captivated by the scent or perfume of plants, the origin of the word perfume, *'per fumum'* – Latin for 'through smoke' – suggests that scents were initially meant for the gods alone. Pride of place of all aromatic scents is the Rose from antiquity to the present day. Recorded in the wall paintings of the Egyptians, roses have been cultivated by various peoples over at least the last 6000 years. Fossils of recognisable rose flowers are known from deposits in the Southern USA dating to about 25 millions years ago.

Rosewater has long been used in many countries to flavour sweet dishes, cakes and wine. Rose petals have been used to make jam and generations of children have been given Rose Hip Syrup for its vitamin C content. The Apothecary's Rose, *Rosa gallica var. officinalis* was named for its use in treating sore throats, its use in eye drops, as well as being used in confections and conserves.

One of the first raw materials which every aspiring perfumer is forced to study at the very beginning of his or her training is the rose, the indispensable pillar upon which perfumery is founded.

The rose, recognised as the queen of flowers, with its romantic history in fairy tales, in art, literature, and music over the millennia, has sparked and inspired human imagination. The rose is synonymous with beauty and love, and a passionate inspiration for the writer's creation of 'Spirit of the Rose', a perfume to complement the birth of rose breeder extraordinaire, Ronnie Rawlins' exciting new scented rose 'Spirit of the Rose'; timed to perfection to complement the launch of this beautiful book, Spirit of the Rose.

The rose has been used in perfumery since ancient times, an Arab legend tells how in the tenth century, pilgrims returning from Mecca admired the scent and beauty of the damask rose, *Rosa x damascena*. The highly scented rose is cultivated and grown in Turkey, Bulgaria, and Morocco. The other noted rose species is *Rosa x centifolia*, also known as Rose de Mai, especially with growers around the town of Grasse near Nice in the South of France and known as the birthplace of modern perfumery.

Early records credit Avicenna (980-1037), an Arab physician, philosopher, scientist, poet and statesman for being the first to produce rose water by the technique of distillation. Today, the major supplier of rose oil is Turkey. In 2003, from some 5000 metric tonnes of rose petals, a total of 1,500 kilos of rose oil was produced. The crop in Bulgaria of around 3,500 metric tonnes yielded about 1000 kilos of rose oil.

Since only 2-3 grammes of rose oil can be obtained from 10 kilos of rose petals, it is one of the most expensive oils in perfumery. Price is the only limit to the use of rose in fine perfumery, however even a trace amount in a formula can soften, give a velvety body, and transform a composition.

The writer of this chapter of the book was inspired by the very first perfume of François Coty, named after a noted mid-eighteenth century French rose, 'La Rose Jacqueminot' of 1903, to create the original signature scent of the Royal National Rose Society, 'Society Rose', a beautiful scent of nostalgia. The very first flaçon of this perfume was presented to the actress and star of To the Manor Born, Miss Penelope Keith, who opened the Society's annual Rose Festival in 1987.

The art and craft of the perfumer is to capture the alluring scents from the flowers and blossoms, create and compose, blend and dispense their precious essences into bottles. Interestingly, sight and colour can be defined, hearing and touch measured, but the sense of smell more difficult to describe; scent is also subjective.

Rosarians all over the world will perhaps never agree on the scent of a particular rose. There are roses heady with fruity hints of peach, apple, apricot, raspberry; citrus notes of lemon, grapefruit, lime; honeyed tones of myrrh, rich tea notes. Many roses exude the odour of moss, cut grass, or leafy green hues, others the scent of spices, perhaps a touch of nutmeg, cinnamon, cloves, woody, velvety and violet, musky, the powdery note of face powder. The spectrum of scent from the roses is almost endless and as wide as the palette of colours.

Finally, I give a tribute to two eminent rosarians, both wonderful mentors who have given pleasure and inspiration to the writer's love of the rose. The late Jack Harkness, who also inspired the design of a twin Rose logo when I founded my boutique perfumery, The Perfumer's Guild Limited, and the rosarian ambassador *par excellence*, Dick Balfour, MBE DHM. What better tribute to commend the reader to seek out his very own rose, 'Dick's Delight', and 'Della Balfour', named for his wonderful wife – rosarians in the true Spirit of the Rose.

Irish Melodies

Thomas Moore

Irish poet, musician and songwriter

*You may break, you may shatter the
Vase if you will,*

*But the scent of the roses will hang
Round it still*

Thomas Moore

A Man for all Seasons

Audrey Balderstone

A profile of the Reverend William McMillan MBE, MA, ML (GCA)

Poetry in perpetual motion seems an apt way to describe Reverend William McMillan. His energy and enthusiasm for everything he tackles is legendary, with poetry tumbling from his lips as easily as artistry flows from his fingers.

Ecclesiastic, lecturer and author are just some of the attributes of the professional life of this extraordinary man. Add to those his keen interest in, and knowledge of, plants and their history, along with his work as an International Demonstrator for the National Association of Flower Arrangement Societies and you realise that here is a man of many parts. Indeed 'Rev Mac', as he is affectionately known, has been labelled 'A Man for all Seasons'.

None of these listings, however, conveys the essence of the man; his wit, his wisdom, his kindness; his joy of life; his immense talent, his legendary generosity; his unique personality. Evidence of some of the facets of his character can be gleaned from the many accolades heaped upon him, and they give a glimpse of the high regard in which he is held by his peers and, indeed, by all who come into contact with him.

Few know that Mac was awarded the Albert Schweitzer Award for his work in promoting religious freedom, but most know of the even higher award which came from Her Majesty, Queen Elizabeth, when he was awarded the MBE in 1999 for services to charity. Years before that, the National Association of Flower Arrangement Societies had made him a 'Special Associate of Honour' in recognition of his services to the organisation, and for his extensive fund-raising for charities throughout the United Kingdom and Ireland, in lieu of fees. In 2003 The Garden Clubs of America conferred on him their highest award when he was made a Member at Large – one of only four non-Americans to be granted this prestigious honour.

Wherever he goes, Mac makes friends. Whether in International Floral Art competitions, where he has won numerous awards, including the coveted 'Best in Show' award at the World Show in Toronto, or representing Ireland in the Flower Festival in Canterbury Cathedral to celebrate four hundred years of Christianity, Mac's humour acts like a magnet. In the midst of all the humour however, Mac manages to create designs that often move his audience to tears, and this was nowhere more apparent than in the crypt of the Cathedral, which he was asked to decorate in plant material – but using no flowers. Few will forget the moving and evocative display of mosses and plant materials, which conveyed the beginnings of Christianity in England.

At home in Ireland, where he has designed many festivals and shows, Mac's greatest success perhaps was the International Design Symposium he master-minded in the year 2000. At that time floral artists from all over the world flocked to a Roman Catholic Missionary College in the beautiful Kingdom of Mourne to decorate the house, attend workshops and demonstrations and stage a Flower Festival. As well as raising thousands of pounds for charity this event was also the culmination of many of Mac's cross-community and interdenominational efforts held throughout Ireland.

In great demand at home and abroad for his ability to keep audiences entertained with a unique blend of floral interpretive skills, knowledge of plant material, poetry and side-splitting humour, Mac, however, remains self-deprecating and humble. Although his art seems effortless he is one who puts his heart and soul into every aspect of what he does. His love of plant material is matched only by the respect he has for those who risked life and limb to bring the rare and the lovely from foreign lands to these shores. Mac is never happier than when working in his garden, or sharing with others his knowledge of the great wealth of plant material which it is our privilege to enjoy.

Lauded by his peers, loved by his audiences, appreciated by his congregation, Mac's feet, however, are kept firmly on the ground by his wife and four children. They all share his wonderful sense of humour and delight in taking him down a peg or two when they think the occasion demands it. It goes without saying that in spite of this they are immensely proud of all he has accomplished and Mac is the first to say that he could not do it without the support of his wife, Sheila and their children.

Like a rose, Mac's personality and art are sure to bring a smile to the lips, perfume to the occasion, a lift to the heart and beauty to the darkest corner.

Sir Thomas and Lady Dixon Park

Text by Spirit of the Rose

City of Belfast International Rose Garden

The Sir Thomas and Lady Dixon Park is one of the most popular parks in Belfast. Spread over 128 acres, bounded to the west by the River Lagan, the park has been in public ownership since 1959 when it was gifted to the Belfast Corporation by Lady Edith Stewart-Dixon. Her Will read: 'To use the said house and lands for the greatest good of the citizens of the City of Belfast'. The gift was to perpetuate the long association of her husband, Sir Thomas Dixon, and herself, with the City of Belfast. The park was named Sir Thomas and Lady Dixon Park.

The estate at Wilmont was formed in the mid-18th Century by William Stewart whose family were prominent farmers. Thomas Jackson, who was one of Ireland's most important Victorian architects, designed Wilmont House itself.

Sir Thomas and Lady Dixon Park today incorporates many horticultural features including the world famous rose displays. Since the early 1960's International Rose Trials have been held in the park and associated display gardens planted. After comprehensive and dramatic redevelopment, the City of Belfast International Rose Garden opened in 1990.

The park now boasts a spectacular range of display areas, historical and heritage sections, trial beds, sympathetic landscaping incorporating mature specimen trees, copse and woodland and up to 45,000 rose bushes, an amazing increase from 35,000 just ten years ago, their scent filling the air during the warm summers.

The idea of a rose trial ground in Northern Ireland was first mooted by Sam McGredy, of the famous Portadown rose firm Samuel McGredy & Son. The Sir Thomas and Lady Dixon Park was chosen as an ideal setting and the first roses were planted in the winter of 1964/65, including entries for Trial 1, 1965/66.

The Rose Society of Northern Ireland was formed in March 1964 and many roses that initially featured in the trials have gained worldwide recognition. A heritage section highlights the roses bred by the McGredy and Dickson families, two of the provinces top rose breeders. Both have won gold medals for their roses all over the world and although Sam McGredy has now moved to New Zealand there are still links with the province.

The rose trials attract approximately 40 new varieties each year and judging takes place five times over the trial sections. Attributes such as habit and growth, fragrance, resistance to disease and flower quality are taken into consideration. Rose Week coincides with the final judging. A programme of events incorporating demonstrations and the Summer Rose and Flower Show ensure that anyone with an interest in horticulture, flowers and nature cannot fail to be moved by the sheer abundance of variety and colour set before them.

Footpaths echo in the memory
Down the passage which we did not take
Towards the door we never opened
Into the rose-garden

T.S. Eliot
Four Quartets 'Burnt Norton'

89

A Thorn on my Side

Eugene Trainor

Extracts from a talk dedicated to the memory of my parents

I was asked in 1993 to assume management of the International Rose Garden at Sir Thomas and Lady Dixon Park just outside Belfast. As a horticulturist loving all plants, I wondered why I had been chosen. But looking back on my life, roses had always been present.

During a talk in London at the Royal Horticultural Society, a note was handed to Sean McCann, the eminent rosarian: "The past is history, the future is a mystery, the moment now is a gift – and that is why it is called 'the present'"

It was, I believe, a statement to validate a love of roses – new and old. The great gift of today is that we can select the best from the new without any need to reject all the wonderful roses that already exist. We can also keep looking forward to being presented with wonderful new roses – a marriage between new and old. Some work better than others.

International Rose Gardens and Trial grounds around the world give us all the opportunity to enjoy roses and see old, new and potential varieties growing side by side. It also enables the rose breeder to consider the best environment – weather, location, and soil condition, for its fledgling to grow.

The City of Belfast International Rose Garden is home to 45,000 roses in a beautiful setting and the staff take a great deal of pride in the gardens, ensuring that they look their best at all times of the year, particularly during the summer months. It takes a lot of patience to deadhead so many blooms! The gardens not only give me great pleasure but have also afforded me a wonderful opportunity of meeting so many dedicated people and travel all over the world to experience other gardens.

Roses now play a significant part in my life but I would like to share a story from childhood, where the rose also made its mark on me. As a child, my brothers and I would pick roses from a very old rose bush in the garden. The rose was white with a beautiful scent and we would take the roses one by one to our mother who would sit and arrange them.

On one occasion our mother was not at her table and, told she had gone in to premature labour, we all prayed for a very long time. To this day we believe that Saint Therese of Lisieux, the little flower of Jesus, heard us for our mother and newborn sister survived. The rose bush was eventually lost when renovation work was being carried out.

In 2001, following the death of my father and a number of years after my mother passed away, I found the print of Saint Therese which used to hang in our home. It was a little battered but under the image was an entire piece about her, one extract being

*'I will spend my time in heaven doing good upon earth
After my death I shall let fall a shower of roses.'*

In May 2001, the same year many people made a pilgrimage to Armagh to touch the Reliquary, a beautifully decorated casket, containing the bones of St Theresa and thousands of roses were brought, to be placed on family graves for special blessing.

One month after, whilst working in the family orchard, we found that the rose bush from which we had picked flowers all those years ago had reappeared. It now takes pride of place in my own garden. The rose has been identified as *Rosa x alba* Pompom Blanc Parfait, its origin being France c1876.

St Theresa herself was born in France in 1873 and I like to think that she grew up surrounded by that very same variety that I held in my hand on the day my sister was born!

Tipperary and Cork

Theresa Collins

Dorothy Graves Garden

The long, hot summer was still with us, but whilst it was close to the end of the season for roses, this did not deter any of us as we gathered in the beautiful country garden of Dorothy Graves in perfect summer weather.

Ballintemple, situated five miles from historic Cashel, is a place of quiet seclusion and beauty, set in the rich farmland of County Tipperary, where Dorothy has lovingly planted and developed the garden over 40 years. Her collection of Old Roses is enviable and this rural idyll provides a true home for them. The bed of wonderful 'Queen Elizabeth' roses, still in haphazard bloom, was complemented by the under-planting of asters in a riot of blues and pinks. Dorothy had cultivated these roses from cuttings taken from a plant her late mother had purchased for 'three and sixpence'. That parent plant survives to this day.

We were happy to welcome David and Annie and to be associated with this project. We set the scene for the pictures with the help of Dorothy and Kay Beardmore.

From my own garden I had picked what I could find so late in the season. I love the character of the roses that ease us into autumn and bravely continue to bloom until the frosts. The strong yellow rose is the reliable and perfect *R.*

'Amber Queen', purchased from a great rose grower in Tipperary, Pat Slattery of Cahir who has spent a lifetime cultivating roses. In our arrangement, this award-winning rose is mixed with other unnamed blooms, including a delicate pale pink rambling rose I cultivated from a hedgerow cutting taken in South Kilkenny. This vigorous plant with an evocative scent of an old rose, blooms over a long period. Among other roses used is the pink 'Constance Spry'.

Every stage of the blooming of a rose is fascinating, from bud to petal fall, and it was so appealing to see David's logo of the rose petal. The roses we used that day fell quite naturally, adding charm to the setting. I had chosen to use Rossa Pottery as its earthy colours and textures complemented the roses well. Each piece originates from the clays of Tipperary and is creatively crafted in a family pottery by Alan and Sarah Walsh in Cashel.

The backdrop of the next photograph is a view of the garden through the 'Beech Summerhouse' – the oldest feature in Dorothy's garden. I used part of my collection of old enamel containers to suit the mood. The setting, using Dorothy's worktable and chair, was enhanced by her story of the precious secateurs included in the picture. These she had received as a Runner-up prize in the Pot-et-Fleur Class at the NAFAS National Competitions in Bath held in the late 1970s. These are a cherished possession and have happy memories for Dorothy as they had been presented to her by Julia Clements OBE VMH. The vibrant pink shrub rose in the picture flowers with abandon and nowadays is used in many roadside plantings throughout the county. I am unsure of the variety.

We concluded the photographs with Queen Elizabeth Roses in an old rose bowl. As the butterflies hovered on the nearby *Sedum spectabile*, this wistful scene captured the peace and beauty of the garden.

Cork – Southern Ireland

Elma Moore's garden

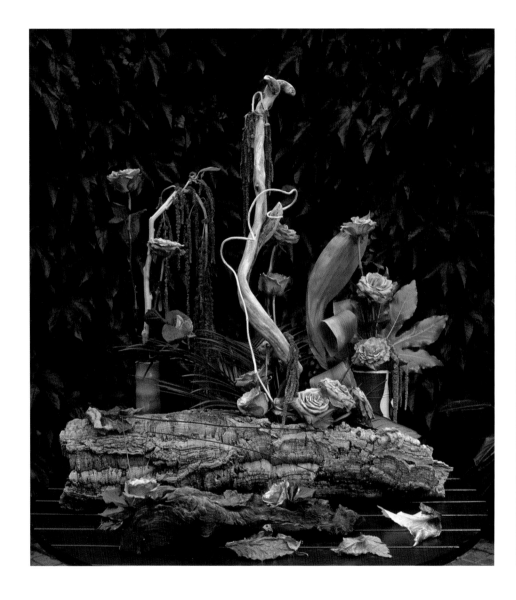

Then bring me showers of roses, bring,
And shed them round me while I sing;
Great Bacchus! In thy hallowed shade,
With some celestial, glowing maid,
While gales of roses round me rise,
In perfume sweetened by her sighs
I'll bill and twine in early dance,
Commingling soul with every glance!

Thomas Moore

The Last Rose of Summer

Thomas Moore

Irish poet, musician and songwriter

'Tis the last rose of summer
  Left blooming alone;
All her lovely companions
  Are faded and gone;
No flower of her kindred,
  No rosebud is nigh,
To reflect back her blushes,
  To give sigh for sigh.

I'll not leave thee, thou lone one,
  To pine on the stem;
Since the lovely are sleeping,
  Go sleep thou with them.
Thus kindly I scatter
  Thy leaves o'er the bed,
Where thy mates of the garden
  Lie scentless and dead.

So soon may I follow
  When friendships decay,
And from Love's shining circle
  The gems drop away!
When true hearts lie wither'd
  And fond ones are flown,
Oh! Who would inhabit
  This bleak world alone!

Thomas Moore

Moonlight to Rhapsody

Gerta Roberts

For the Amateur Rose Breeders' Assocation

'The hybridising of plants, either by nature or deliberately by man to produce new varieties, has been happening for centuries.'

For hundreds of years amateur gardeners have been attempting to hybridise new roses. One of the earliest to succeed was the Rev. Pemberton, who in the early 20th century bred a completely new type of rose, the Hybrid Musk. His first, in 1913 was 'Moonlight', which was soon followed by others, 'Penelope, 'Prosperity', 'Cornelia' and several more. These sweet-scented roses are still well known and commercially available.

Here in the United Kingdom today, we have an active and productive Amateur Rose Breeders Association whose members are constantly breeding new varieties with many of their roses now in commerce, not just in this country but also worldwide.

Many gardeners will, I am sure, have heard of the rose "Champagne Cocktail', a delightful cluster-flowered floribunda with a delicious fragrance, raised by Colin Horner in 1985. This pale yellow, medium-sized double flowered rose, splashed with pink, won a gold medal at the International Rose Trials. His most recent winner is the climber 'Golden Future'. Another member, Len Scrivens, has bred the most disease-resistant rose to date, the yellow patio 'Baby Love'; Chris Warner, in 1989, bred the first of a range of climbing miniature roses, 'Warm Welcome'.

Derrick Everitt, Secretary of the Amateur Rose Breeders Association has, as his life's ambition to breed a really brown rose. He has already bred several in very promising, gorgeous colours. In Cardiff, Lionel Poole is working to breed lovely hybrid tea blooms, particularly suited to exhibiting at rose shows.

Ronnie Rawlins has bred many roses and in 2001 launched two at the British Rose Festival at Hampton Court, a white floribunda 'Baby Face' and a yellow shrub 'Desert Orchid'. The editor of the ARBA Annual, Dave Kenny from Eire, hybridised pink 'Riverdance' and a lovely white, pink-edged hybrid tea 'Sister Joan' which has won the top award for fragrance in the International Trials. We are delighted to tell you that Ronnie has now also bred and named a rose 'Spirit of the Rose' inspired by this book. A soft, heavily scented lavender rose, it produced its first few blooms in the summer of 2003.

This brings me to the show-stopping shrub rose 'Rhapsody in Blue' A past President of the Association, Frank Cowlishaw, spent 25 years crossing and re-crossing his seedlings in search of the perfect purple rose. In 2000 this rose won all the major awards in the International New Seedling Rose Trial held at the Royal National Rose Society's Trial Ground at St Albans, Herts.

All our amateur rose breeders have the same burning desire to hybridise roses and to produce even more wonderful new varieties. Many have won awards and medals in International Rose Trials around the world yet despite their competitive spirit and the prestigious awards, members are more than willing to abide by the aims of the Association to share their knowledge and encourage every one to try their hand at hybridising new roses. The Association is not a specialists club, it is open to everybody who has ever (or who has ever wanted to) plant a seed and see what comes up. We are all generous with advice and help and will even suggest 'rosy parents' if you really don't know where or how to start. Do remember, roses are like people, their offspring seedlings are just as different as our offspring. If you cross two roses and produce one rose hip, you will obtain a varying number of seeds, maybe up to 40. Every single seedling rose will be unique, and the blooms will never have been seen before. Isn't that wonderful!

A Life-long Affair with Roses

Diana Joyce

Nestling at the bottom of Watership Down in North Hampshire lies the ancient and picturesque village of Kingsclere where my earliest memories belong. At the back of our house were the water-meadows where as a four year old I would escape, quite hidden from view, into a shoulder high drift of wild flowers.

It was here that my life long affair with roses began, for in the hedgerows, where I could never reach them, grew wild briar roses, all tangled up with brambles and honey-suckle. Through the innocent eyes of a child I believed the rose was the most beautiful flower of all.

Later, when I had grown a little and could reach them, I made futile attempts to concoct perfume from these delicate maidens, boiling them in a tiny saucepan over a toy cooker, storing the extract in a jam jar. Although the resultant brew resembled pickled wasps, there remained a heady, primitive essence that I can still recall to this day. It wasn't until many years later that this love affair with roses would become truly fulfilled. I joined a local evening class to learn about flower arrangement and in the first lesson the tutor showed us how to arrange five roses with their own foliage on a pin holder. I gingerly transported them home and proudly displayed them on the kitchen table. Even wildest imagining could not have prepared me for what was to develop from this simple beginning, a career far beyond my dreams.

At the end of the course I accepted an invitation to give a fund-raising demonstration in our local church hall, for our children's playgroup. The budget was tight so I raided the garden for all possible materials and was able to produce enough roses, foliage and seed-heads for an uncontrived, loose and flowing design in a copper samovar. The small audience was captivated, and I noted their reaction with surprise. Although there were six other designs in the programme, none included roses. So it was from my first demonstration as a beginner, that I became aware of the spirit of the rose and its visual appeal, its power to stir the emotions, and its refined charm. The feedback from the young mums and dads was like a medicine to me. I was smitten.

Gradually my career blossomed, from demonstrating engagements in cosy intimate village halls and grand theatres all around Great Britain, to vast auditoriums in capital cities around the world. Each country has given me a

wealth of experience, each audience never wavering in their appreciation of the rose. From many European Flower Clubs, South Africa, Canada and the USA, the same warm and emotional reaction to the rose prevails.

A demonstration of my dreams would consist of a stage full of old-fashioned roses dripping effortlessly from priceless antique containers, but a balanced programme is necessary, even if too much of a good thing is simply wonderful!

I recall the nervous excitement when purchasing roses from the wholesale market in Johannesburg. I was searching out hot colours in this hot country to interpret Zulu art. I found the brightest cerise, orange, purple and scarlet roses. Assertive young ladies, those, clamouring to be liberated from their straightjacket of cellophane wrapping and taking centre stage. These beauties knew their place – prima donnas all, looking down at the supporting cast with disdain as I massed them together in a riot of colour.

In Fairfax, Virginia, I had the privilege of being escorted around an eminent rose grower's garden to select all the blooms for my forthcoming demonstration. Was I at the gates of Paradise, strolling between arches and bowers festooned with every available species of rose?

Imagine then, on a balmy early October afternoon, just pointing to the blush pink, peach and apricot blooms I required and my distinguished host cutting them for me. Heavily scented and heaven sent all rolled into one. At their most fragile and breathtaking best, those classical beauties required reverent handling if they were to star under the powerful lights of the theatre. But star they did, almost arranging themselves in romantic urns and garlands, in frivolous rococo style.

Of necessity, my work demands meticulous preparation, rehearsal and presentation. I see my role as partly one of striving to help audiences escape for a couple of hours from the mêlée of everyday life, through the visual medium of plant material. But probably my own greatest escape is to create a floral vision, spontaneously and unselfconsciously, without pre-conceived notions or rehearsals. Sometimes it means looking at familiar materials with fresh eyes, re-inventing the old and the familiar, re-discovering what was there all the time, harmoniously assembling the parts. Each design then becomes at one with nature, yet transitory save for the magic eye of the camera.

To attempt a composition consisting of one type of plant material is a real challenge, but possible when one considers the bounty nature has given the rose, from root to stem, thorn, leaf, bud, flower and fruit.

National flower of England the rose may be, but nature, the true artist, gave her personality and character, form and petal formation, colour and perfume, all drawing us like a magnet to a central riveting eye, to the very spirit of the rose.

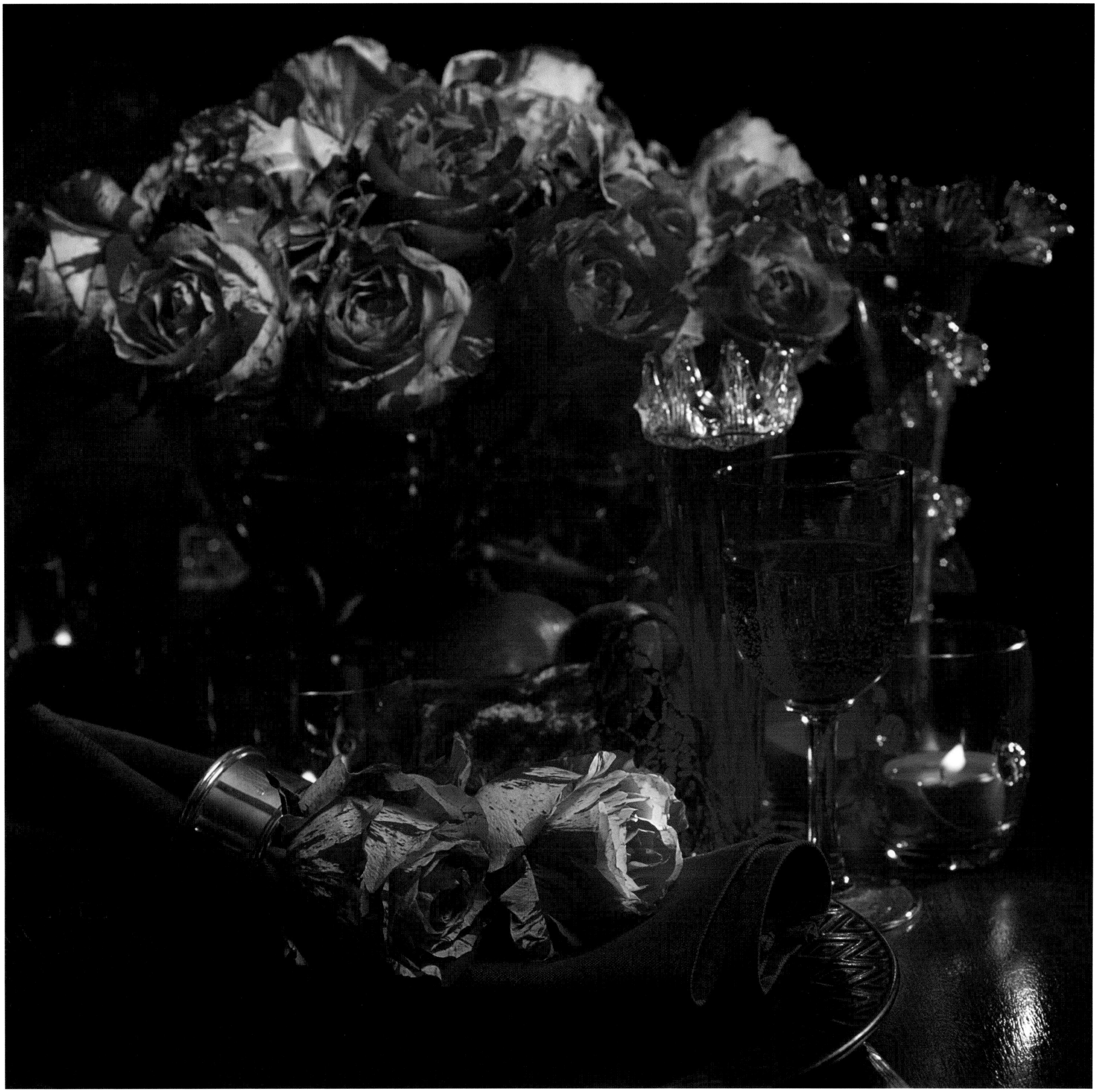

Happy among his Roses...

Jill Grayston

A profile of Rosarian Peter Beales VMH, FI. Hort. DHM

Peter Beales, whose passion for roses was instilled at an early age, moved into horticulture after leaving school. He became apprenticed in 1952 to the famous Rose Breeder and Grower, Edward LeGrice and studied at Burlingham Horticultural College, (now Easton College) in his native Norfolk.

Having learned a great deal about the breeding and growing of roses from his time working under the late rosarian, Graham Stuart Thomas in the late1950s and '60s, Peter founded his own Company, Peter Beales Roses Ltd, in 1968. Subsequently, with the support of his family, he has developed Peter Beales Roses so that today it is one of the leading rose nurseries in the United Kingdom.

His speciality is Classic Shrub Roses, Climbers and Ramblers, the firm having built up a collection of more than 1300 different varieties over the years. The history and evolution of roses is of special interest to Peter, hence his large collection of old Roses, several of which he has saved from extinction. Over the last twenty-five years Peter has bred and introduced some thirty of his own cultivars. His catalogue has become one of the most respected works of reference in the rose world.

His Company exhibit at major shows in the United Kingdom and overseas. Peter designed a stand for a large Exhibition in Tokyo in 2000 and in that same year, won the award for the Best Exhibit of Roses at Hex in Belgium. His firm has won ten Gold Medals and numerous others at the Chelsea Flower Show over the last 32 years. Other Shows where the Company has won prestigious awards are Hampton Court and BBC Gardeners World Live. The stand at Chelsea Flower Show in 1999, designed by his son Richard Beales, also won the 'Lawrence Medal' for the best display at any of the RHS shows during that year.

The Lawrence Medal was again awarded for the Classic Rose Garden display staged at Chelsea Flower Show in 2002. The President's Trophy for the best overall display at Chelsea Flower Show 2003 and The President's Trophy for the best display in the British Rose Growers Show as part of Hampton Court Palace Flower Show were further awards for the Company.

Most recently the Company is proud to have been awarded 'The Williams Memorial Medal' by The Royal Horticultural Society. The Medal is awarded for the best group of plants of any one genus to have shown excellence in cultivation during the year as displayed at The Chelsea Flower Show in 2003 and is to be presented at the Royal Horticultural Society's AGM on 1 July 2004.

Peter has been awarded a number of personal honours for his work with roses: including, in 1996, The Dean Hole Medal, the highest honour from the Royal National Rose Society. In 2000 he was awarded Fellowship of the Institute of Horticulture GB. A further personal award made to Peter Beales is The Victoria Medal of Honour for services to Horticulture, presented at the Society's AGM in the summer of 2003. That year, Peter was also appointed President of the Royal National Rose Society. Peter is a Freeman of the City of London and a Liveryman of the Worshipful Company of Gardeners.

To date, Peter has written four major books on roses, all having been translated into German, French and Italian. Peter also does his own photography. He lectures on roses throughout the world in addition to venues throughout the UK. Notwithstanding his great successes in the rose world, Peter is a quiet, shy man, happiest among the roses in his Norfolk fields or in his modest office set in their midst.

The Rose Garden at Belvoir Castle

Her Grace the Duchess of Rutland

After the birth of our son Charles, the Duke agreed that the Rose Garden at Belvoir could be replanted. The Duke's decision pleased me greatly as I have always had an interest in history and I should now have an opportunity, so I thought, to choose only those roses which were historically correct for the period and that could, at the same time, be planted together to give the gentle effect of having been planted naturally.

There having been a rose garden on the site since the early 1900s, it was clear that the old rose beds were becoming sick, so the first task in restoration was to replace the soil. Whilst the effort of digging out and replenishing the soil was well worthwhile, it seemed like faith moving mountains when our loyal gardener, Mr Kempson worked with such fervour, but eventually the task was completed. As this work was being undertaken, His Grace was assessing which would be the most suitable roses to choose for the garden. All winter we discussed how to select only the varieties which were, in both our opinions, the best embellishment for the Castle.

Although Belvoir Castle was the site of the early experimentation in spring flower bedding, during Victorian and Edwardian times, there were forty-four gardeners to maintain the plans of the 5th Duchess, making the Vale of Belvoir fit into her idea of a picturesque garden surrounding the Castle; today we have but four. The Rose garden is situated near to the site of the famous statues created by Caius Cibber (1680), moved to this position at the behest of the 5th Duchess when she created her garden of the seasons and senses. These seven statues, some of the first ever produced in England, represent the four seasons, taste and touch and Juno with her peacock – the peacock of course representing the Manners family crest. The Duke says I have all her motherly attributes, whenever I remark that I am leaving some gardening to do when the children have grown up!

This project was such a challenge that we consulted many books on roses. The first was 'Roses and Rose Growing' by Rose G. Kingsley. I had previously read her book 'Eversley Gardens' and I felt that this book, written in 1908, would emphasize those roses that would have been in the original garden. The lists of varieties were excellent, but the Duke felt that the moment one walks into a garden there has to be a thirty second feeling of 'I wish to see more of this' or the whole emphasis could change and the boredom factor set in. I was not helping him choose roses purely for my own enjoyment but essentially for the 60,000 visitors we see here at the Castle every year. They need to get the immediate and intense sensation that this is a cared for garden.

Now I will let you into a secret, – one that most professional writers on gardening do not know – and it is this I believe that makes the rose at Belvoir so special and original. I read Mrs Earle's 'Pot Pourri from a Surrey garden'. It is fashionable today to sniff at her views. But I realised that she was born a Villiers with her two younger sisters married to Lord Loch and Lord Lytton and so was in a position to observe the roses that worked. She was accepted in society but never as an equal!

This was the advice she gave almost over one hundred years ago: 'It is well worthwhile to look at a copy of the illustrations of Redouté's 'Les Roses'. Do not underplant too severely, no roses like this and use roses which have stood the test of time.' Here I disagreed a little! She mentioned the rose R. 'Jules Margottin'. This is one of those roses that I consider represents the history of all our garden plants, but seemingly it is no longer available.

There was a little book published at the turn of the 20th century called 'Mary's Meadow', written by Juliana Ewing. The story told of two children who made a little garden in the Squire's meadow with some hose-in-hose cowslips. Eventually the Squire was so taken with the idea that he gave the meadow to Mary; and the only rose that they wished to grow was 'Jules Margottin' for its scent. The book was a phenomenal success and it led to the foundation of the Parkinson Society. John Parkinson wrote one of our greatest gardening books in 1629 where children would go and seek lost garden plants from the previous centuries in old cottage gardens. I realised then that I had to stop what Mrs Earle had elsewhere referred to as 'book gardening' and contact the well-known rosarian and grower Peter Beales who, in my opinion, has the finest understanding of period roses.

I discussed with the Duke the possibility of using certain types of rose and then in greater detail choosing the roses that Peter Beale had selected as suitable for our Rose garden. The Duke made a profound statement: 'A rose is still a rose and the name is not that important. What is important is that the rose should reflect our personal choice'. These were the roses that together we chose for our garden.

Perhaps I gave in too easily to my husband in choosing many roses that were modern and without the sense of history I wished to achieve, but he is correct. Not all our visitors are rosarians; many wish to see the pleasure of a rose in bloom at the time of their visit. The Duke considered it essential to choose repeat flowering types. We have a longstanding tradition here at Belvoir that all visitors are treated with equal care regardless of their knowledge or status.

R. 'Cornelia', introduced in 1925 was my first choice. Its apricot-pink double flowers bloom over a long period and have a scent I find quite delightful. This was counterpoised with 'Penelope', whose dark foliage and stems contrast well with its semi-double creamy pink flowers. This too is repeat flowering.

R. 'Comte de Chambord', although only three feet high, was introduced in 1863. Its gray-green foliage and strongly scented pink flowers always please me. As I write, I recall my friend who grows the pretty violet *Viola* 'Comte de Chambord' with its strongly scented, double white flowers – I must remember to break Mrs Earles' golden rule and just try a small portion beneath this rose one day!

R. 'Veilchenblau' was introduced in 1909. Climbing lazily upwards, its scent is not exciting but its small semi-double trusses of violet-purple frequently cause comment. I always enjoy a change of scent and the apple scent of 'Albéric Barbier', raised in 1900, is sufficiently popular for people to recognise it instantly. Its creamy white flowers, shading to yellow have a good repeat flowering habit. The double creamy-apricot flowers of 'Buff Beauty' continue for much of the summer and, growing up to a height of six feet, the plant does not dominate the garden at the expense of the other roses.

Blooms of 'Ferdinand Pichard' with heavily scented double flowers of pale pink, streaked with crimson, are carried over a long period. There is but one flowering for *R. gallica* 'Versicolor', Fair Rosamund's rose, streaked and splashed in pink with crimson. It has been in our gardens for so long that I could not enjoy the Rose garden without this splash of colour. The same applies to *Rosa x alba* 'Semiplena', with its air of better days. 'William Lobb', with its great moss rose blooms was introduced in 1855. To me, this has everything a Victorian rose garden should contain.

To make sure that flowers would be available to all throughout the visiting season, we added a range of modern hybrids whose flowers carry the feel of *temps perdu*. Roses like 'Awakening', 'Sir Frederick Ashton', 'Attleborough' and 'Chevy Chase' mixed well with 'John Cabot' and 'Sally Holmes' helping 'Frensham', 'Grüss an Aachen' and 'Ballerina' keep the colours vibrant throughout the season.

This selection provides a suitable contrast to the statues, which carry the structure of the rose garden throughout the year. If the connoisseur does not consider them to be sufficiently smart, I would say that once the children are grown I may replant but for the moment I am satisfied that we have achieved a garden whose welcome is apparent to all visitors. In this the Duke is well pleased.

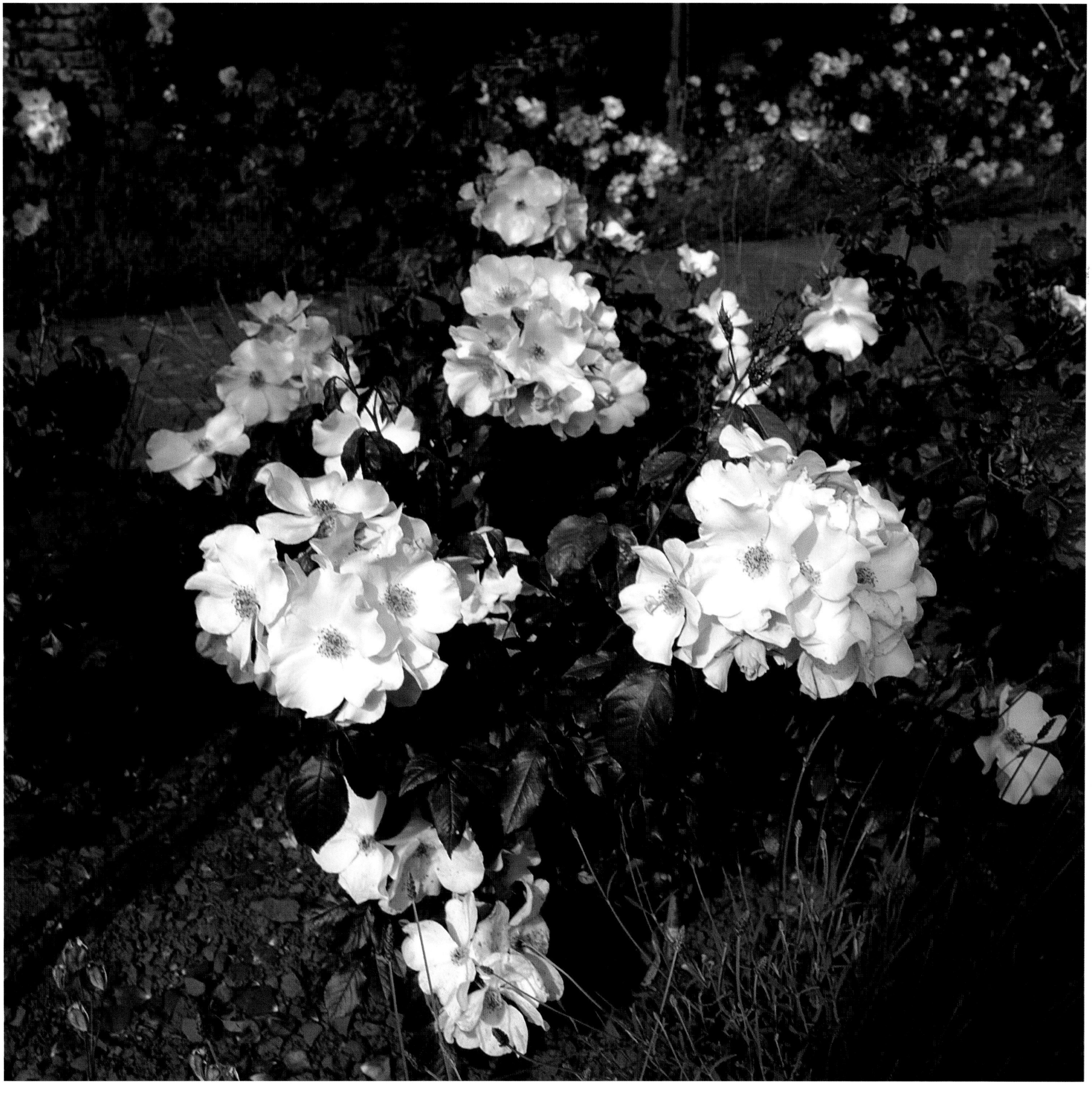

114

Inspired by the Language of Flowers

Judith Derby NDSF AIFD FSF

My love of flowers began as a very young child, living in the country and spending hours walking in the fields, where wild orchids, and numerous other flowers sprang up each year. My favourite flowers were the wild roses that covered the hedges, and I loved to pick some to take home to my Grandmother. It was the memories of her face when she took the posy of roses from me that thirty years later gave me the inspiration for my business card at the time I opened my first florist shop; it was simply inscribed, "Give Flowers, give Pleasure".

The language of flowers has been very important in my life as a flower arranger and florist. For Valentine's Day that bouquet of red roses says 'I love you'. I remember clearly one order I had to fulfil was for a single red rose lying on a bed of black lace! Deep red roses are said to mean 'bashful' and 'shame'. 'Forgive my foolish timid ways!' Yellow roses may signify jealousy! Deep pink roses are for the bride, a message from the bridegroom saying, 'Charming, I am bewitched and enchanted by your beauty' or pure white roses, a sign of purity and innocence, 'I am worthy of you'.

It is fair to assume that roses existed before man, and have been used throughout time as a means of expressing thoughts and feelings. A message sent without words, just in the language of the flowers, bringing joy and comfort, happiness and hope to all who receive them.

> *'In eastern lands they talk in flowers,*
> *And they tell in a garland their loves and cares;*
> *Each blossom that blooms in their garden bowers*
> *On its leaves a mystical language wears'.*

Unknown

I have had many opportunities to use this knowledge, both professionally and in a non-professional manner! Life did begin at 40 when I opened the first of my two florist shops! I consider myself fortunate to have worked with such a fascinating medium, and have many wonderful memories of floral experiences. On one occasion I was requested to provide all the flower arrangements for a visit by Princess Anne, and to design a basket for a dog to present to her!! We had great fun in the shop deciding what sort of basket would be most suitable, and after much argument, resorted to one of the girls crawling around on the floor with a basket in her mouth! After several replacement baskets, as the dog kept chewing it up, on the week of the visit they finally found a dog that behaved! Princess Anne stood in amazement as the dog walked right across the arena with the basket in its mouth and stood before her as she took it out of its mouth!

Having lived in the Vale of Belvoir all my life, I had been a regular visitor to Belvoir Castle, and I was delighted to be asked by the Duchess of Rutland to design and stage a Flower Festival, together with the Council and all members of the North Midlands Area of NAFAS. Following from that success, the next year I was invited to organise a 'Floral Extravaganza'. My aim was to bring together both flower arrangers and florists to stage a design of their choice within a specific area, but allowing them the freedom to create a showcase of floral art and professional floristry.

I invited top designers from all over the United Kingdom; their response was overwhelming. Many hours were spent at the Castle deciding just how many arrangers we could accommodate, and in which areas. Companies were invited to attend the event and also for sponsorship of designers for demonstrations and awards. We had two well-known demonstrators, one sponsored by Smithers-Oasis U.K. Ltd and the other sponsored by The Society of Floristry. Both featured the history of the Castle with innovative use of plant materials, artistry and skill in their portrayal of the theme. Events like this don't just happen, as anyone who has organised such an occasion will tell you. Hours and hours are spent going over each little detail, to make sure all goes smoothly. My reward and that of my two helpers, was the congratulations and thanks of all who attended, and who said what a pleasure it had been to stage in such a magnificent setting and in such a friendly atmosphere. Once again the language of the flowers had spoken to all who had visited and had taken part.

The Language of Flowers was never more important to me than when I attended the sixth world show (WAFA) in Durban South Africa in 1999. My chosen class was "Metamorphosis" so when I interpreted the 'The Life Cycle of a Butterfly', I felt it was vital to use the plant material in different ways, in natural and in a contrived form, to interpret the title in all aspects. The result for all the time spent researching the life of a butterfly; A Gold Medal.

Flowers have spoken more than I can say in written words and it has been a great privilege to be involved with this book, even in just a small way. David Lloyd is a true artist, and his passion for roses shines through, so I hope you will let the pictures speak to you, in the same way as they do to me each day.

117

A White Rose

John Boyle O'Reilly

The red rose whispers of passion,
And the white rose breathes of love,
O, the red rose is a falcon,
and the white rose is a dove.

But I send you a cream-white rosebud
With a flush on its petal tips;
For the love that is purest and sweetest
Has a kiss of desire on the lips.

John Boyle O'Reilly

121

The Legacy of the House of Cocker

Dr Tommy Cairns

James Cocker & Sons. A family of rose breeders with dreams, courage and purpose

Scotsman, Dr Tommy Cairns, President of the American Rose Society has kindly given us permission to include extracts from his fascinating, illustrated lecture on the James Cocker dynasty, delivered to the World Rose Convention at Glasgow in 2003.

The beginning of James Cocker & Sons of Aberdeen Scotland in 1841 was due to an irreconcilable disagreement between head gardener, James Cocker (1807-1880) at Castle Fraser in Aberdeenshire and the Laird. Being of strong religious beliefs, James refused to pick fruit on the Sabbath, indicating to the Laird that he was willing to pick fruit until darkness fell on Saturday evening, but not on a Sunday. To no avail, the compromise failed and James left his employment, starting up his own business at Sunnypark Nurseries in 1841.

As the business prospered, James took his son (also named James) into partnership and extended his business by opening an additional nursery site at Morningfield. With ideal soil conditions for growing roses, father and son went on to win their fair share of rose awards. After the death of the founding patriarch, son James (1832-1897) took his three sons (William, James, and Alexander) into the business assuming the present day title in 1882 of James Cocker & Sons. In the 1890s their rose breeding effort resulted in the company's first important rose, 'Mrs Cocker', winning a National Rose Society Gold Medal. In 1913 'Mrs Andrew Carnegie' also won a NRS Gold Medal.

In 1902 the nurseries at Springhill were expanded to 62 acres.... In 1915 William Cocker died and Alexander headed the company as sole proprietor until his death in 1920 leaving his 13 year-old son Alec (Alexander Morison Cocker) as heir. Three years later the trustees closed the nursery... Young Alec left school to serve an apprenticeship in general horticulture. However, in 1931, he had a motorcycle accident suffering multiple fractures to his right leg, leaving it permanently damaged. Alec re-established the business as a general nursery and later fell in love and married Anne Gowans Rennie. In 1952 they jointly decided to specialise in roses – a decision the rose world would later applaud many times over! In 1959 a 70-acre site at Whitemyres was purchased and soon greenhouses appeared to undertake rose breeding in a serious manner!

Alec and Anne forged a bright career move gaining national and international recognition in the years that ensued. By the late 1960s their breeding programmes resulted in many notable varieties such as 'Morning Jewel', 'White Cockade', 'Rosy Mantle' and 'Alec's Red'. In 1975 Her Majesty Queen Elizabeth II granted a Royal Warrant to James Cocker & Sons as suppliers of her roses. Then fate dealt an undeserving blow to this noble family so dedicated to growing the best roses. Shortly after the spectacular introduction of 'Silver Jubilee' at Chelsea flower show in 1977, Alec died suddenly at home at the age of 71.

His wife, Anne, and their teenage son Alec have carried on the family tradition in the 21st century with yet another generation of Cockers... Since 1978 they have introduced almost 100 varieties, building upon the rose breeding programme initiated in the 1960s by Alec Cocker as well as extending into other classifications. Anne and Alec adopted some favourite seedlings into their breeding lines, such as the seedling, ('Sabine' x 'Circus'). In 2001 the family was awarded their second Royal Warrant from Her Majesty Queen Elizabeth The Queen Mother. The Cockers have enjoyed a long tradition of producing prize-winning roses... It could be said that Alec Cocker built the rose foundations and Anne and Alec the superstructure that is today 'The Legacy of the House of Cocker'...

Family patriarch James Cocker and his son James, were responsible for contributing to rose breeding and plant inheritance during the 19th century with the formal introduction of four registered varieties: 'Duchess of Fife', 'Mrs Cocker', 'Christian Curle' and 'Mrs Andrew Carnegie'. However, his grandson, Alec and wife Anne during the 20th century were accountable for making the family name a household word within the rose world. During his lifetime in rose breeding Alec Cocker achieved so much progress within the short span of years intensely devoted to his dreams. In that golden decade Alec registered thirty-six varieties.

For Alec Cocker the goals in his rose breeding demanded disease resistance as a primary quality. Using a number of shrubs and species known to possess resistance to fungal diseases, Alec developed a number of seedlings with wonderful qualities such as clean foliage... Numerous crosses from a repeat flowering seedling developed from 'Clare Grammerstoff' x 'Fruhlingsmorgan', as well as many 'Picasso' seedlings, were used in his breeding programme to develop hybrid tea type blooms.

Alec Cocker and the late Jack Harkness were kindred spirits forming a unique bond of friendship, sharing notes and theories as well as exchanging seedlings for evaluation. In particular, Alec Cocker wanted to breed with *H. persica* because of its attractive red eye. Unable to track down a plant within the UK, Alec ordered seeds from Iran. Then, on a visit to Jack Harkness in Hitchin, Alec commented that the soil was ideal to grow *H. persica*. Thereupon, Alec willingly gave Jack half of the imported seeds from Iran – an act of generosity not often credited to a Scot! But then that gift of seeds is yet another great rose story for another annual on Jack's experiences with *H. persica*.

... Alec was blessed with great success producing such magnificent varieties as 'Alec's Red' ('Fragrant Cloud x Dame de Coeur') awarded the Edland

Memorial Medal for fragrance in 1969 as well as the NRS President's International Trophy and Gold Medal in 1970. From 'Alec's Red' as a seed parent came forth 'Hot Pewter' and 'Radcliffe Flame'. Equally successful was the light vermilion rose floribunda 'Anne Cocker', an upright and vigorous plant with… long-lasting blooms as a cut flower. Alec's own favourite was 'Rob Roy'. While named to celebrate a famous Scotsman of the 17th century, Alec was amused to receive a request from his French agent for the written permission of Mr Rob Roy to proceed with trade-marking.

In America, New Zealand and Australia the popularity of 'Playboy' as a top floribunda for showing and for breeding was explosive, becoming one of the most sought after varieties. From 'Playboy' as a seed parent have resulted such American favourites as 'Playgirl' by Ralph Moore, 'Flutterbye', 'Scentimental' and 'Betty Boop' by Carruth. Alec's introduction of 'Silver Jubilee' gave the world of rose breeders a true genetic treasure trove to be explored! The latest edition of Modern Roses lists about 80 progeny from 'Silver Jubilee' as both seed and pollen parent, to such great varieties as 'Lincoln Cathedral', 'Dave Hessayon', 'Lovely Lady', 'Don Charlton', 'Savoy Hotel', 'Mike Thompson', 'Audrey Hepburn', 'Abbeyfield Rose', 'Fyvie Castle', 'Angela Lansbury' and 'Queen Charlotte'.

Alec, however, was denied seeing his creations become the favourites of rose growers all over the world. Just before his passing, he commented that one of his greatest pleasures was being assisted in crossing and budding, by his young son, Alexander, the fifth generation of the family. Thankfully, Alec Cocker was accorded recognition for his pioneering work in rose breeding before his death in 1977. He was awarded the Scottish Horticultural Medal and the RNRS Queen Mary Commendation Medal. The late Jack Harkness in his 1977 obituary said of Alec, 'For many rosarians, life without Alec Cocker will never be quite the same. He was inflexible in purpose and principle, wise, industrious, kind, hospitable and very humorous. A very splendid man has gone away.'

With equal vigour his wife, Anne, with their son Alexander 'Alec' have continued the mark of excellence in rose breeding into the late 20th and early 21st centuries. … they have taken Alec Cocker's dreams to a higher level, having introduced almost one hundred varieties since 1978.

During the last few decades the Cocker family has named roses for various charities, namely a light pink HT 'Caring For You' commissioned by the Church of Scotland with a donation of £1.50 per plant to assist the social work of the church. 'Gwen Mayor' was named to honour an outstanding teacher at Dunblane Primary School and here again a donation of £1.50 per plant is for artistic, cultural, musical and sporting events to benefit all primary schools in Scotland. More recently, a new Cocker floribunda has been selected by the RNRS named 'Sunsplash' to mark the occasion of the 13th World Rose Convention held in Glasgow, July 2003.

… Roses bred by the Cocker family grow equally well in Aberdeen as they do in Studio City, (California), Portland (Oregon), Melbourne (Australia), Hamilton (New Zealand), Osaka (Japan), Bombay (India), Cape Town (South Africa), Buenos Aires (Argentina), Paris (France), Rome (Italy) etc. For this is the true essence of rose endurance of 'The Legacy of the House of Cocker' – gifts for the world to share, to remember, and most of all to enjoy!

The Thistle and the Rose

The year 2003 marked the 400th Anniversary of the union of England with Scotland.

The conflict between England and Scotland ended with the Union of the Crowns in 1603. King James I wrote and talked in the Scottish language yet authorised the translation of the Bible into English for the benefit of all. That edition was published in 1611. The number of words used in the translation was one third of that used in all Shakespeare's works.

James I's own book on witchcraft, a subject he detested, was called 'Daemonologie' and became so it is said, the inspiration for Shakespeare's 'Macbeth'.

In 1707, the Parliaments of England and Scotland were joined, and so began the United Kingdom. It is also interesting to note that circa 1881/83 William Morris produced a fabric and wallpaper that he entitled 'The Rose and Thistle'. One of Charles Rennie Mackintosh's favourite icons in his designs was the rose.

O, my love is like a red, red rose,
That's newly sprung in June.
O my love is like the melody,
That's sweetly play'd in tune.

As fair art thou, my bonny lass,
So deep in love am I,
And I will love thee still my dear,

Til all the seas run dry.
Til all the seas run dry, my dear,
And the rocks melt wi' the sun!
And I will love thee still, my dear,
While the sands o'life shall run.

And fare thee well, my only love,
And fare thee well a while!
And I will come again, my love,
Though it were ten thousand mile!

A Red Red Rose – Robert Burns

129

'The Rose is the Flower of Flowers'

Shirley Monckton

Inscription in the Chapter House of York Minster

The Greeks and Romans used roses in profusion. Garland makers, florists of their time, created garlands to adorn the triumphant standards of their armies and they were worn on the heads of merrymakers. Garlands were also hung on altars and over doorways to celebrate or symbolize an important event, such as the birth of a child. Garlands were made with small bunches or clusters of flowers tied together, then bound into long lengths. There are few examples of flower arrangements of those times, but there is a wonderful mosaic at the Villa Quintilii on the Appian Way, from the second century AD that shows a basket of mixed flowers, included in which are several roses. Certainly the ancients revered the rose and considered it the most evocative and beautiful of flowers.

For those who enjoy the art of arranging flowers, the rose is one of the most used and loved. It never fails to bring a special dimension to any design. It will stand alone in a simple glass vase revealing untold delights as its bud gradually unfolds. It may be made into a simple posy or arranged as the perfect companion for almost any other type of flower or foliage. Many people prefer to keep their roses firmly in the garden, but they are missing the opportunity to savour both the perfume and the visual delight in the form of cut flowers.

The many varieties of rose provide an unlimited source of inspiration for the flower arranger. They can be used to create a variety of moods with styles ranging from the simplest informal arrangement to the grand and opulent. For example, old garden roses may portray romance whilst the bright vibrant modern hybrids can be used to produce the most stunning floral sculptures. The floral paintings of the Dutch masters frequently incorporated wonderful Bourbon and Moss roses in their still life arrangements, often depicting the equally beautiful reverse side of the flower.

Within the many species there is an incredible diversity of size, form, colour and texture. Some roses possess an elegant and classical beauty and produce just a few large single blooms, others, like the wild dog-rose, ramble indiscriminately over all that stands in its path giving an abundance of flowers. Rose growers have provided an Aladdin's cave of jewelled delights from which to choose and the plethora of colours can sometimes be quite overwhelming. Whilst some may not appeal as a garden shrub, as a cut flower they are a real joy to include in a floral design.

A marvellous florist rose called "Illusion" is unusual in that the colour of its flower differs at each stage of maturity. When opening it presents as a green gradually turning cream and then developing into a warm yet vibrant pink. The beauty for the floral designer is that once the rose is cut the colour will remain unchanged and, even if cut when fully open, it is very long lasting.

It is advisable to cut roses from the garden early morning or late afternoon, preferably not in full sun or when very wet. Also consider how the shrub will look after you have cut it. Pick perfect blooms, some partially opened, but most in bud. Cutting old roses should be an easier task as the shrub should be larger and produce an abundance of flowers.

'Conditioning' cut or bought roses will enable them to survive longer and give the best performance possible. 'Conditioning' is the name given to preparing flowers and foliage for use in arranging. Roses need a little more care than other flowers and plant materials. A drooping rose head can often be prevented by placing the cut stem ends in very hot water for about twenty seconds and then giving them a long cool drink in a bucket for a few hours. This seemingly drastic treatment is used to remove the air lock that forms when the flower is cut (the flower does this naturally as a means of self-preservation). If this air lock is not unblocked the water will not be able to travel up the stem and the result; a dead flower. Try this method if the flowers appear a little tired. It may not always be possible to give the 'hot water' treatment but the minimum of conditioning should be to cut the stems at an angle and to place them in cool water for at least two hours. It is courting disaster to pick or buy and arrange straight away.

Drying roses is another age-old practice. Sand was originally used to draw out the moisture, but modern techniques have brought many new methods. Commercially dried roses are good, but drying your own favourite types and unusual coloured flowers can be rewarding. Silica gel or 'Flower Dry' are just two of the many types of drying agents that can be used, instructions for their use are always included in the packets. Probably the most critical point about drying roses is the time factor and this is usually a matter of trial and error! Too short a time and the rose will wither and too long in the mixture will create brittle flowers and the petals will drop quickly. Disappointments will happen, but the successes will far outweigh them and the joy of the extended life of such treasures is well worth it. Pot-pourri is yet another way to enjoy the treasures so freely given by the rose.

Often called the "Queen of Flowers", it should perhaps follow that the rose must always be arranged in the grandest of vases or urns. The rose however does not expect such extravagant treatment. A cascading design of roses arranged in profusion in a silver bowl lit with candles is indeed beautiful, but the rose will give pleasure in almost any container whether glass or celadon, wood or alabaster. Whatever container you choose the rose will enhance it and its spirit will bring all that is needed to the design, it is indeed the flower of flowers.

135

Contemporary Floral Design

Carol Hunter

Connect Design Group was formed in 1997 to further contemporary trends in floral art and design and to cater for keen flower arrangers who wished to develop their creativity. Currently we have approximately sixty members who meet in Ross-on-Wye, Herefordshire four or five times a year. Members are encouraged to participate in day schools and workshops rather than just attending flower arranging demonstrations. The Group organizes and stages exhibitions of contemporary floral art, many members also competing in major flower arranging competitions, often with great success.

Tutors are invited from all over Britain and from overseas to teach new and innovative methods, sharing the latest trends from their part of the world. We also aim to stimulate interest in allied art forms and it was with this in mind that we invited David Lloyd to present a workshop on how best to photograph floral exhibits. Members staged designs featuring roses, after which David spoke about the importance of good lighting, background effects, suitable formats and choice of photographic equipment. David then photographed the designs, as did those members who had brought their cameras and were keen to try out the techniques they had learnt.

We had chosen to use roses as these flowers offer the floral designer a wide range of hues with which to work and have the added advantage of being available from florists and wholesalers at any time of the year. In contemporary design, many parts of the rose are used – flowers, leaves, thorny stems and rose hips all of which give interesting form, colour and texture. With new varieties of cut roses being developed all the time, opportunities are endless.

Of the cut blooms available from the florist, white roses such as *R.* 'Akito' or 'Bianca' are extensively used for elegant or dramatic effect, while cream is always popular, providing a rich and opulent appearance. The cream *R.* 'Prophyta' is a good example. Yellow comes into its own when trying to bring a little dazzle and brightness into an arrangement with *R.* 'Illios' and 'April' being two of the most outstanding varieties. Pink is a favourite with many floral designers and the beautiful clear pink hues of roses such as *R.* 'Esperance' or 'Noblese' add a touch of glamour to any arrangement. Blooms in shades of peach or apricot add a warm glow and look wonderful when teamed with blue-green foliage. Vibrant and zingy orange certainly grabs attention, clashing colours frequently being used in contemporary design.

A palette of reds from crimson, carmine and magenta through to the orange vermilion shades including scarlet and cinnabar, add excitement. Red is an advancing colour and boldly holds the eye. Bi-coloured roses appear in many fascinating combinations allowing the designer to experiment with exciting way-out combinations.

The variety of texture and form in rose blooms offers wonderful opportunities for innovation in floral art. Stems are used quite frequently, stripped of all leaves, to create structures in which to compose up-to-the-minute designs. In autumn, rose hips are much prized for their shiny, glossy almost jewel-like appearance, giving a superb seasonal dimension to flower arranging.

Seeking Perfection

Deborah Hutton

A judge's perspective

The exercise of judgement is always hard. And it is never harder than when subjective elements have to be added to the objective assessment of adherence to rules or specifications contained in a schedule. Thus competitive floral art cannot fail to present a judge with serious challenges. On the one hand, he or she must monitor observance of the guidelines laid down to a very strict standard whilst, on the other, looking for that extra spark of initiative and creativity that takes a garden or a floral arrangement just that little bit closer to perfection.

The judges at our great horticultural shows, such as those organised by the Royal Horticultural Society at Chelsea, Hampton Court and Tatton Park, can call on many years of experience not only as judges but also, in most cases, as exhibitors of long-standing. However experience does not make their eventual decisions any easier. First, they must check the quality of plant material used in the exhibit: it must be free of pests and diseases and show no signs of damage. Then the space or stand should be well filled, but not to the point of appearing crowded – 'there should be room for the butterflies to fly', as the saying goes. Labels or title cards should be appropriate, accurate and well presented, but not overly dominant. In a planted exhibit there should be unusual or difficult-to-grow specimens: if the exhibit is presented as a garden, one should not be able to see signs of pots plunged into the growing medium. If the display is of a single genus it should contain a wide representation of the variations shown by the genus in cultivation. The finish of the exhibit must be well groomed and have an overall freshness, while the display's design should enhance the appearance of the plant material used. Of course, the exhibit must conform to the Show Schedule or the relevant Manual.

Then comes the subjective part of the assessment, it is relatively easy for a judge to tell, from the way that colour, texture, form and space have been used, whether or not the artist has a good knowledge of the elements and principles of design. The judge will look for a good contrast of textures and form, the creation and use of space within and around the design, the horizontal, vertical and overall balance, for a colour-scheme that brings harmony to the whole, thus creating a satisfying effect. Also, a good sense of proportion and scale while any accessories used should make a valid contribution to the interpretation. The predominance of plant material over all the other components is paramount. Finally, the judge will hope to feel a *frisson* of excitement when viewing the design that exhibits all these features coupled with artistic merit that will distinguish it from its competitors in its class.

Most of the factors which enter into the judge's assessment, apply to all forms of exhibit, whether they are stalls showing garden accessories or displaying plants and flowers of outstanding beauty. While different judges may attach varying weights to particular elements of these criteria, it is astonishing how rarely there is disagreement between them over the final decisions.

Between the National Association of Flower Arrangement Societies (NAFAS) and the Royal Horticultural Society, the regulations governing the judging of shows differ in certain respects. For NAFAS shows, for example, enhancement of plant material, unless specifically excluded in the schedule, is permitted; the RHS takes the opposite view. To illustrate one of these aspects, the subtle use of artificial colouring on driftwood or other plant material, provided that it is applied with skill and has relevance to the subject, would not be a matter for concern by NAFAS, but would be considered unacceptable by the RHS. Neither RHS nor NAFAS judges use a points system, but both organisations ensure that their judges undertake a deliberate process of weighing all the criteria mentioned above. What both sets of judges – indeed all judges – have in common is the hope that an exhibit will cause them to gasp with pleasure at having come across a display showing perfect plant material with innovation, harmonious use of the principles and elements of design and a blend of colour that sends messages of mood and stirs the emotions of the onlooker. Then, and only then, can a judge's dream of finding perfection be realised.

The Design Element

Neil Whittaker NDSF AIFD FSF

When Neil was asked to contribute designs for 'Spirit of the Rose', he considered it a challenge to do so with just one species of flower, the rose, albeit one of the most beautiful and fragrant flowers in the world!

He hopes that his brief, to create individual designs interpreting a gift, a corporate celebration and modern living, has been accomplished with the use of techniques from traditional to the most up to the minute, and that they will inspire and excite readers.

Neil takes particular pleasure in pushing forward the boundaries of floral design and floristry techniques to better understand why, where and how plant materials grow, to gain insight into the characteristics and natural form of blooms, including roses and to show these wonderful flowers at their best.

Whilst his day-to-day work is undertaken from his Manchester base 'The Design Element', a business he has co-owned for over twenty-one years, Neil may also be found in many parts of the world demonstrating and sharing a wealth of knowledge in his chosen art form. In the competitive world, his successes include being Runner-up at the first world floristry championships in Manilla in 2000, which event was followed by many television appearances and, in 2003, winning the coveted Chelsea gold medal for professional floristry.

Neil believes that whether you work with just one or with many varieties of flower material, if you allow your mind to stretch and find new boundaries, innovative designs will come straight from the heart.

Neil thanks his partner Anthony Williams ICSF FSF and their staff, who have all contributed to this wonderful project. He also thanks the FTA (Flower Trades Association) for the most stunning roses supplied and David Lloyd for this inspirational challenge and opportunity to show his love of this spectacular flower, the rose.

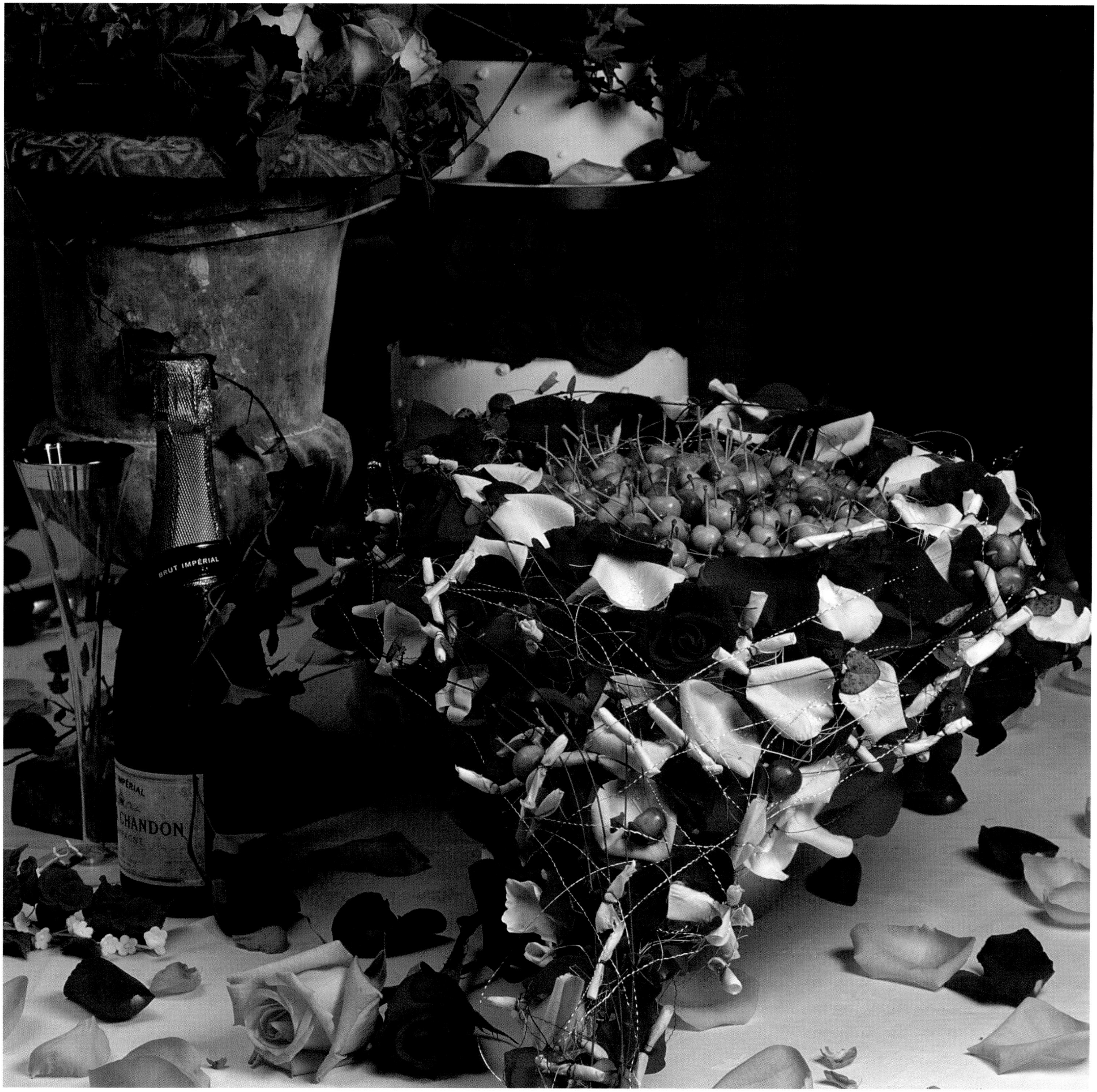
BRUT IMPÉRIAL
CHANDON

144

145

Aphrodite's Rose

Serena Helene Smith

Aphrodite's Rose Essences are named after the Greek Goddess of Love. They embody the purity and perfection of the rose. The rose is symbolic of earthly and spiritual love. It is both innocent and seductive, delicate, yet strong. The rose is the flower of romance, seduction, femininity and youthfulness.

The healing qualities of roses have been written of since before the 1st century. They have many proven medicinal properties and are particularly helpful in healing and balancing all aspects of the reproductive system. They also calm the nervous system and encourage the regeneration of cell growth.

'The rose distils a healing balm
the beating pulse of pain to calm'
 Anacreon

On an emotional level, the rose will help us become more nurturing, aware and confident, for it also symbolises our connection to the Divine. Good health requires not only an awareness of what makes a healthy body, but healthy emotions too.

The essences are based in the purest organic rosewater. Rosewater is cooling and aids the digestive system. It is an excellent tonic for grief, bereavement and depression. It is safe taken internally and is prepared for us by a well-known herbalist who cares passionately about the methods used in distilling his rosewater. A small amount of organic vodka is added to each bottle to preserve the contents.

The essences are made from roses grown in areas protected from pollution and where the air is pure. The gardens, surrounded by hills, provide sanctuary to many forms of flora and fauna.

Aphrodite's Rose Essences are different because they also draw upon the ancient science and philosophy of colour healing. Each colour rose has its own unique effects and can be used for healing and balancing as well as for stimulating deeper levels of consciousness. We all instinctively know or feel which colour will benefit us at any given time.

Passion – Red

This vibrant red rose essence is said to generate a sense of inner security. It will help you become motivated and courageous, giving you back your passion for life.

Joy – Orange

Orange rose essence promotes an abundance of vitality and enthusiasm. It acts on the senses, influencing emotions, desires and pleasures and is particularly beneficial for those who feel cut off emotionally. The colour orange brings a sense of freedom from limitation.

Clarity – Yellow, red tinged

The yellow tinged-red rose represents fire, which burns off our negative thoughts and feelings. It helps us to become more aware and gives us the ability to sense and feel the emotions of others. The colour yellow encourages new ideas coupled with wisdom.

Infinite love – Pink

This exquisite pink rose essence was made under a starry sky, by the light of the full moon. Both the moon and the rose are symbols of the feminine. This essence opens the heart so that one can become more nurturing and feel safe to give unconditional love. The colour pink helps to soften and expand the heart.

Inner beauty – Cream tinged pink

These creamy roses tinged with pale pink were offering themselves for this essence. The perfectly formed buds speak of beauty within, allowing us to open up to fully express ourselves. It helps us to appreciate our own beauty and to love ourselves as part of the Divine.

Intuition – Mauve, violet and purple

A riot of mauve, purple and violet roses was used for this essence. It will open us up to the creative forces in the higher dimensions and bring us a sense of trust and inner 'knowing' that all is well.

Bouquet – mixed

This essence is made from all the above roses and brings balance and harmony to the mind, body and spirit, helping us to feel at one with the Universe.

Cleopatra's Milk Bath
One half a cup of organic olive oil
10 drops organic essential oil of geranium
6 drops essential oil rose maroc
Dried rose petals
Organic milk powder

Mix olive oil with geranium and rose oil
Pour onto milk powder, mix thoroughly
Add dried rose petals and stir well
Pour into glass containers and seal

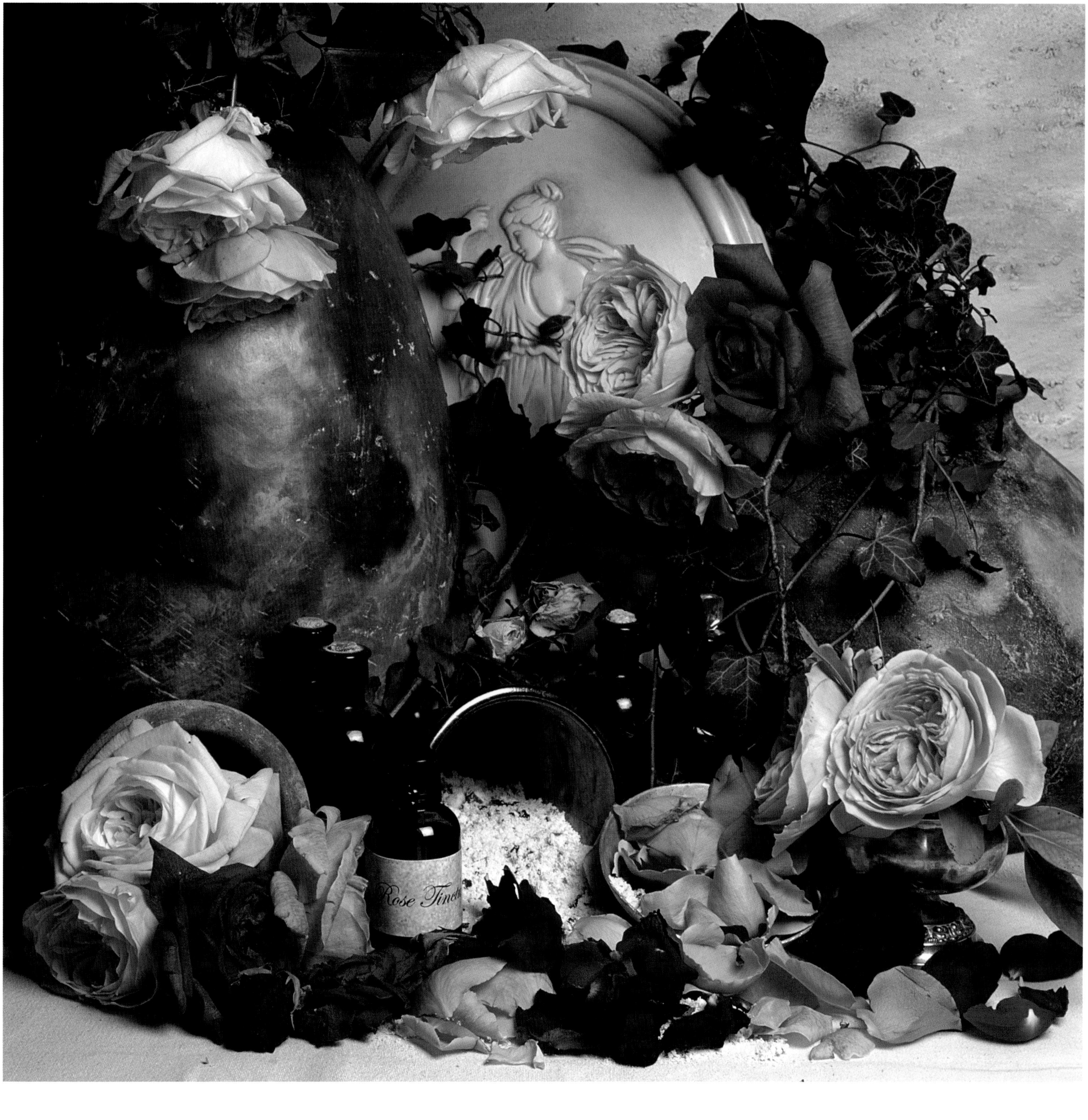
Rose

RHS Garden, Rosemoor

In addition to the diversity of its landscape, Devon plays host to a magnificent selection of fine gardens, with surprisingly variable climates. This diversity is wonderfully expressed at RHS Garden Rosemoor, a garden rich in variety and year-round interest, recognised last year by being awarded the accolade South West 'Large Visitor Attraction of the Year 2003'.

Situated on the west-facing slopes of the beautiful Torridge Valley, the Garden has become one of the jewels in the West Country crown, as well as becoming a garden of national importance. Originally the grounds of a fishing lodge, the Garden was first developed by Lady Anne Berry, until she gave the Garden to the Society in 1988. Lady Anne's Garden is still very much in evidence. It is a plantsman's garden of specimens collected from all over Europe, Australia, New Zealand, Papua New Guinea, Japan, the USA and temperate South America. When Rosemoor was given to the RHS, it took a green field site below the road running through the Garden and created a totally new formal garden, featuring two Rose Gardens, the Square Garden, the Spiral Garden, Potager, Herb and Cottage Gardens, Foliage & Plantsman's Garden, lake and stream, a Winter Garden and three model gardens. Rosemoor is now one of the most exciting and inspiring gardens you can visit in Devon, and is particularly famous for its stunning collection of roses. When you look at how well the garden is established today, it is hard to believe that almost two-thirds of it is fourteen years old or less.

Rosemoor is acclaimed by gardeners throughout the world, but you do not have to be a keen gardener to appreciate the Garden's beauty and diversity. Whatever the season, the Garden is a unique and enchanting place that people return to time and time again to gain ideas and inspiration or simply for a relaxing day out. The Formal Garden reveals a wide range of plants and planting styles in a series of individual garden 'rooms', with lots of ideas to inspire visitors for their own gardens. Major attractions include the Queen Mother's Rose Garden for modern roses, and its companion the Shrub Rose Garden containing 130 varieties. A delightful small Alpine display house, opened in 2002, provides colour and interest all year round. The two colour theme gardens provide strong contrasts: the Spiral Garden has cool and pastel flowers while the Square Garden contains searing hot coloured plantings. The Cottage and Herb Gardens are more informal in style, separated by the Potager with its decorative vegetable planting. Leaf form and colour dominate in the Foliage Garden; while the Winter Garden is full of interest during the colder months. Finally, the Model Gardens demonstrate three contrasting design solutions for the average domestic plot. Other attractions include the Stream and Bog Garden and Lake; a richly planted Fruit and Vegetable Garden; large areas of parkland and arboretum. Newly developed woodland walks offer interesting glimpses of local wildlife and wild flowers.

One of the main purposes of Rosemoor is to demonstrate to gardeners what can be grown in the West Country, where the perceived wisdom was that roses grew poorly. The RHS researched which plants might grow well under local conditions, checking our selections with a number of noted rose experts, before arriving at their final choice of around 200 cultivars. The combination of careful choice allied to thorough preparation and aftercare has resulted since 1990 in a superb annual display of modern, shrub and old-fashioned roses throughout the garden. Their confidence in the long-term future of roses at Rosemoor can be seen in the investment of considerable time and effort in the upgrading and refurbishment of both major rose gardens, the Queen Mother's Rose Garden (for modern roses) in 2001/2, and the Shrub Rose Garden in 2003/4.

In addition to the charms of the garden itself, Rosemoor runs an exciting and diverse series of events for adults and children and is building a reputation for hosting some of the West Country's finest art and craft exhibitions. The NCCPG Plant Sale, Bonsai Weekend, Rose Sunday, Family Weekend and Apple Day are just some of the highlights in the 2004 calendar. In September, just as the early autumn evenings are drawing in and you are looking for something to do after the rush of the summer, Rosemoor's Autumn Festival, provides the perfect tonic. The two-week festival features music, arts and crafts and food alongside a range of horticultural events.

If you haven't had a chance to visit Rosemoor yet, it really is time you did. You will be astonished to discover a horticultural oasis hiding behind the Garden's high hedges. Step inside the Garden, and you will know that you have discovered somewhere very special to which you will want to return time and time again.

153

It was the Time of Roses

Thomas Hood

It was not in the winter
Our loving lot was cast:
It was the time of roses –
We plucked them as we passed!

That churlish season never frowned
On early lover yet!
O, no – the world was newly crowned
With flowers, when we first met.

'Twas twilight, and I bade you go,
But still you held me fast:
It was the time of roses –
We plucked them as we passed ...

Thomas Hood

The Real Flower Company

Rosebie Morton's personal story of English roses

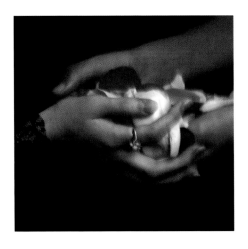

If I think back to my childhood, I was about five years old when gardens started to mean more than just a playground. The pleasure of burying one's nose in a Margaret Merrill Rose and being overcome by its scent is a memory that will stay with me forever. It may well be this lasting impression that inspired me to create the Real Flower Company.

My mother has been a major influence in my obsession with roses. As my father was in the army, we were only ever in a house for a couple of years but despite this mother somehow managed to create a garden which could both inspire and delight even the most uninformed of onlookers. The sight of Constance Spry in full bloom, New Dawn showering the front of the house or Albertine's coppery blooms scenting the air are all clear images in my mind.

I started my own garden when I married Matthew in 1988. The excitement was immense because we had a clean canvas to do with whatever we wished and that, as far as I was concerned, meant roses in every shape and form. Margaret Merril found herself in the bed by the backdoor so any excuse to head for the garden involved passing her and getting a fix of that incredible scent and ethereal beauty. Evelyn, Iceberg, Chapeau de Napoleon, Bonica, Little White Pet, Cécile Brunner all followed. Mermaid made her presence known over the back door and Caroline Testout found herself on the front of the house along with New Dawn and Mme Alfred Carrier. Over the next five years other characters entered the stage all taking different roles be it through their sheer beauty, or functionality as a screen for some utilitarian object. My role was proud director of my cast and I really did become besotted with them!

Roses are so incredibly diverse as a species. They have so much to offer within a garden. Their foliages alone are astonishing, picture the sight of Oranges and Lemons on a crisp day with the sun shining on its glossy red leaves. *Rosa glauca (Rosa rubrifolia)* which has either plum-purple foliage in sun or slate-grey in shade and tiny pink flowers which smother its arched branches and then turn to scarlet hips, is the perfect foil for other roses. Roseraie de L'Hay has wonderful green foliage but also displays blooms with sumptuous scent. I am always overwhelmed seeing *Rosa sericea pteracantha* with its beautiful red thorns along the stem. I planted it so that it would catch the early morning sun and make an arresting sight.

The myriad of assorted colours, their different habits and flower shapes, all offer the gardener such a wonderful choice. The extraordinary parchment colour of Julia's rose, for instance, was once described as 'elderly ladies underwear washed with tea'! The striped blooms of Purple Tiger have always fascinated me with no two blooms ever the same. Scent is undoubtedly a significant factor in my love of roses. To have scents ranging from almond to vanilla, musk to tea, blackcurrant through to lemon never ceases to amaze me. I could be discussing wines but roses offer all these characteristics and more.

When we sell our roses as cut flowers at Farmers' Markets, we find that customers treat our stand as a 'Fragrance experience' and come to savour the scents. People love to take their time enjoying this simple pleasure, one often missed in modern times. What really brings it home to me is how their faces literally light up with sheer joy with the experience and very often the memories that the roses recall. People often say why don't roses smell as they used to? This statement has provided the real purpose to my crusade to reintroduce this simple but underused pleasure to as many people as possible. Our retail side of the business sending bouquets throughout the United Kingdom has also led to the creation of a large file full of letters from customers exclaiming the joy they have experienced with our scented roses.

I am absolutely passionate about roses. There is always something new to experience with roses and they never cease to bring me pleasure. The scent is uplifting, the wealth of colours invigorating. I feel that as a species, with all they contribute, they deserve their place as Britain's most popular flower.

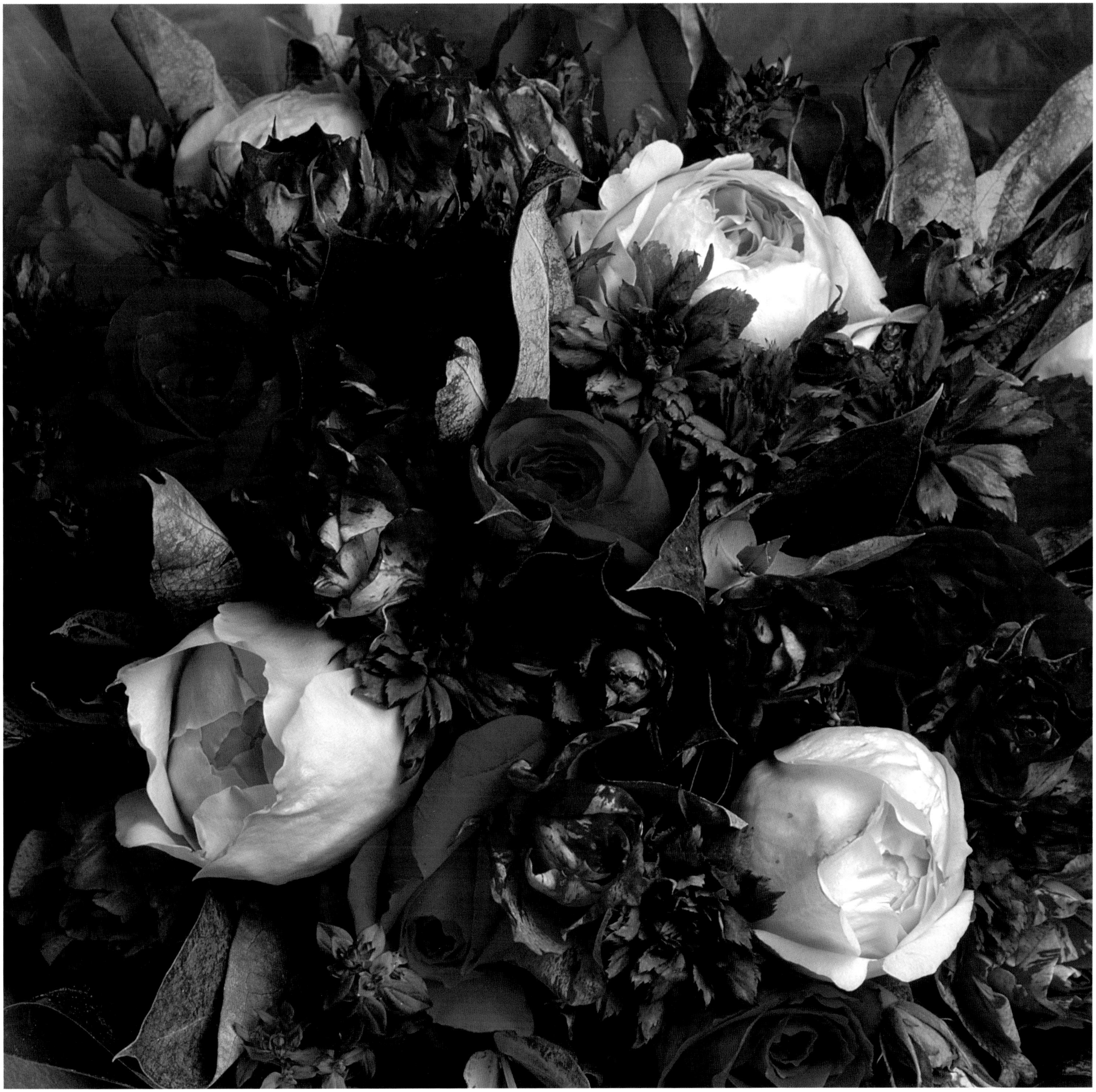

The Sensual Rose

Anne Finch, Lady Winchilsea

My hand delights to trace unusual things,
And deviated from the known and common way'
Nor will in fading silks compose
Faintly the inimitable rose.

Anne Finch, Lady Winchilsea (1661-1720)

163

Index of featured roses

164

Index of featured roses
(continued)

List of Contributors

Austin, David
Michael Marriott
David Austin Roses Limited
Bowling Green Lane
Albrighton
Wolverhampton WV7 3HB
Tel: 01902 376300
www.davidaustinroses.com

Bailey, John - Artisan Perfumer
Founder of The Perfumers Guild Limited
Tel: 01923 260502
parfumjohn@aol.com

Balderstone, Audrey
abalderstone@btconnect.com

Balfour, R C. MBE DHM
Past President The Royal National Rose Society
President Emeritus The World Federation of Rose Societies
Past Master The Worshipful Company of Gardeners

Beales, Peter
Peter Beales Roses
London Road
Attleborough
Norfolk NR17 1AY
Tel: 01953 454707
www.classicroses.co.uk

Blunt, Anne - Floral Designer

Bowyer, Michael
The Flower Cellar
2b Nursery Road
Salisbury SP2 7HX
Tel: 01722 416144
www.flower-cellar.co.uk

Cairns, Dr Tommy
President of the World Rose Federation
c/o James Cocker and Sons
Whitemyres
Lang Stracht
Aberdeen AB15 6XH
Scotland

Cakes, Wedding
Richard's Cakes
Urmston
Manchester

Cocker, Alec
James Cocker and Sons
Whitemyres
Lang Stracht
Aberdeen AB15 6XH
Tel: 01224 313261
www.roses.uk.com

Collier, Barbara - Floral Designer
Bloomsbury,
46 Southern Road
Camberley GU15 3QL
Tel: 01276 506167

Collins, Theresa
President of the Association of Irish Floral Artists
Gortnaceare
Brookville
Tipperary Town
Ireland
Tel: 062 51857
theresamcollins@eircom.net.

Columbian Flowers
UK. Information office
The Ward House
Clifton Road
Kingston KT2 6PZ
Tel: 020 85496549
info@columbianflowers.co.uk

Derby, Judith NDSF AIFD FSF
International Floral Designer,
Demonstrator, Tutor and Judge
Tel: 01476 870414

Joyce, Diana - International Floral Designer

Grayston, Jill - Freelance Journalist & Editor books & magazines
Member, Garden Writers' Guild
JAGrayston@aol.com

Dixon Park, Sir Thomas and Lady
The City of Belfast International Rose Garden
Upper Malone Road
Dunmurry
Belfast,
Northern Ireland
Tel: 02890 320202

Floristry, The Society of
www.societyoffloristry.org

Edwards, Susie
Floral Designer & Decorator,
Demonstrator, Speaker, Teacher,
Writer. Consultant
www.susie-edwards.co.uk

Hutton, Deborah
International Floral Designer,
Demonstrator and Judge.

The Royal Horticultural Society Garden
Rosemoor
Great Torrington
Devon EX38 8PH
Tel: 01805 624067
www.rhs.org.uk

Gawsworth Hall
Macclesfield
Cheshire SKU 9RN
Tel: 01260 223456

Grey, Barry
International Floral Decorator and
Designer
Tel: 01260 270665

Hair and Make-up by Kathryn
UBeauty
Urmston
Manchester

Hunter, Carol
Connect Design Group

Jackson, Jean
Designer Bridalwear
14 Station Road
Urmston
Manchester M41 9JN
Tel: 0161 7482878

Johnson, Edna
NAFAS Associate of Honour
International Judge, Demonstrator,
Teacher of Floral Design & Flower
Arrangement and RHS Speaker
Tel: 01494 673505

Kitt, Malcolm
Floral Decor Limited
Floral Decor House
Douglas Road
Cork
Ireland
Tel: 021 4292944

Knights, Julia NDSF FSF

Lindley Library
Royal Horticultural Society
80 Vincent Square
London SW1P 2PE
Tel: 0207 8213100

Maidment, Hilary
The Old House
161 Wilton Road
Salisbury SP2 7JQ

Marriott, Michael
(see David Austin)

Mathews, Joanne and Peter
The Manorhey Hotel
Urmston
Manchester M41 9LT
Tel: 0161 7483896

Magowan, Anna
The Royal National Rose Society
The Gardens of the Rose
Chiswell Green
St Albans
Hertfordshire AL2 3NR

McMillan, The Reverend William,
MBE, MA
Minister of Religion of the Non-
subscribing Presbyterian Church of
Ireland
Dunmurry
Belfast
Northern Ireland

Monckton, Shirley
Author and Flower Arranger

Morton, Rosebie
The Real Flower Company
Units 1 and 2 Durleigh Marsh Farm
Petersfield
Hampshire GU31 5AX
Tel: 08704 036548
www.realflowers.co.uk

NAFAS
National Association of Flower
Arrangement Societies
Osborne House
12 Devonshire Square
London EC2M 4TE
Tel: 0207 2475567
www.nafas.org.uk

Pollard, Ian and Barbara
Abbey House Gardens
Malmesbury
Wiltshire SN16 9AS
Tel: 01666 822212
www.abbeyhousegardens.co.uk

Pygmy Pinetum Nurseries
Cannop
Royal Forest of Dean
Glos GL16 7EQ
Tel: 01594 833398

Rawlins, Ronnie, Amateur Rose
Breeder
The Fairway
Fixby
Nr Huddersfield
West Yorkshire
HD2 2HU
Tel: 01484 315566

Roberts, Mike and Gerta
The Amateur Rose Breeders Assoc.
Keepers Cottage
Little Barney
Fakenham
Norfolk NR21 ONL
106565.345@compuserve.com

Rosa Floral Designs
4 Wesley Walk
High Street
Witney Oxford
Tel: 01993 771177

Rose Revived, The
Newbridge
Witney
Oxford
Tel: 01865 300221

Rutland, The Duchess of Belvoir
Castle
Grantham
Leicestershire NG32 1PE
Tel: 01476 871002
www.belvoircastle.com

Smith, Serena Helene
Flower Essence Practitioner
Aphrodite's Rose
PO Box 3896
London NW3 7DS
www.aphroditesrose.com

Sudeley Castle
Winchcombe
Gloucestershire
GL54 5JD
Tel 01242 604357
marketing@sudeley.org.uk

Toller, Tony
Trustee and Director of The Rose
Theatre Trust
21 New Globe Walk
London SE1 9DT

Trainor, Eugene - Horticulturist and
Rosarian
Parks and Amenities
Belfast City Council
The Cecil Ward Building
4-10 Linenhall Street
Belfast BT2 8BP

Vaughan, Sally
Theatre producer

Whittaker, Neil NDFS A1FD FSF
The Design Element
Flowers with Passion and Style
67 Liverpool Street
Irlam
Manchester M44 6E
www.thedesignelement.co.uk

Willow Tea Room
217 Sauchiehall Street
Glasgow G2 3EX Scotland

York , Susannah
Actress and Patron of The Rose
Theatre Trust

167